THE HOLY SPIRIT: THE HELPER WE ALL NEED

by

Frederick K.C. Price, D.D.

FAITH ONE
PUBLISHING
LOS ANGELES, CALIFORNIA

5th Printing

The Holy Spirit: The Helper We All Need
ISBN 1-883798-18-3
Copyright © 1996 by
Frederick K.C. Price, D.D.
P.O. Box 90000
Los Angeles, CA 90009

Published by Faith One Publishing
7901 South Vermont Avenue
Los Angeles, California 90044

Contents

Introduction

I believe that we, as children of God, are at the threshold of something new and more exciting than we have ever experienced before. I believe that the Body of Christ is coming into a higher level of spiritual awareness, and we should be expecting greater things to occur as the Father God entrusts us with more of His ability and more of His revelation.

However, in order to move to that greater level of spiritual awareness, and for those greater things to occur, we need to have supernatural power. We need to have something that will allow us to move as God intended the Church to move from the beginning. That "something" — that power — is the Holy Spirit.

But who is the Holy Spirit, really? The people who lived at the time the King James Bible was written, back in the early 17th century, thought of a spirit or ghost as something intangible, something that could not be contacted physically. Therefore, the translators of the King James Bible used the term "Holy Ghost." When you hear the word *ghost*, you may automatically think of Casper the friendly ghost, floating around the room and passing through walls. That is not what the Holy Spirit is really like at all.

There are varying ideas about the third person of the Holy Trinity. One idea promulgated by a particular religious organization is that He is an inanimate force (like the force of gravity or the force of magnetism) that flows from God to move His servants to do His will. You cannot see gravity or magnetism, but you can see what happens as those forces operate.

What is interesting, however, is how inconsistent this organization really is about this concept. This group has printed its own translation of the Bible, and in that translation, it uses personal pronouns to describe the Holy Spirit. You generally do not use personal pronouns, such as He or Him, to describe an inanimate force.

You yourself may have wondered about this entity called the "Holy Spirit" or "Holy Ghost" and thought, "Who or what is He?" We know about Jesus, and have seen so-called pictures of Him. We can see Michelangelo's concept of God (as an elderly gentleman with a long beard and big muscles) in the frescoes he painted in the Sistine Chapel. At least, we do have some sort of caricatures of Christ and the Father God, but who has seen a picture of the Holy Spirit to give us some idea of what He looks like?

The simplest thing for us to do is to let the Bible paint us a picture of the Holy Spirit, and go by what it shows us. In this book, we are going to look at what the Bible says about the Holy Spirit — about who He really is, and what He is here to do for us, both individually and as members in the corporate Body of Christ.

God does nothing in this earth-realm except through the Holy Spirit, and the Holy Spirit operates through the Body of Christ — the Church. The Body of Christ without the Holy Spirit is like a physical body without a spirit in it. When a person's spirit and soul leave his or her physical body, we have what is called physical death. That person's physical body does not move, talk, breathe, function, or grow, because that person's spirit is what animated his physical body.

Likewise, the Body of Christ is made up of many members, but the Holy Spirit is who animates the Body and empowers it to do the will of God. We need to know who and what the Holy Spirit is, so we can cooperate with Him, and do God's will to the best of our ability.

1

The Person of the Holy Spirit — Part 1

The first thing I want to discuss is the fact that the Holy Spirit is really a person, a divine person. He is on the same level as God the Father and Christ Jesus, and like God the Father and Jesus, He is a distinct personality. Yet all three of these distinct individuals comprise the one and only true God.

This is not as complex a concept as it may sound, and it is entirely scriptural. In Genesis 5:1-2, we have this statement:

> This is the book of the genealogy of Adam. In the day that God created man, He made him in the likeness of God.
> He created them male and female, and blessed them and called them Mankind in the day they were created.

God uses the singular and the plural together in this verse because "Mankind" is actually the name for man in general. Man and woman are of the species "Mankind." They are both called Mankind, yet they are plural because they are separate persons, and they have separate personalities and functions. According to the above scriptures, we can say Mankind is one, yet he is two.

In the same sense, God is one, yet He is three — Father, Son and Holy Spirit — and all through the Bible, there are references that indicate this plurality. The most famous of these references is in Genesis 1:26, which states, **Then God said, "Let Us make man in Our image, according to Our likeness...."** *Us* and *Our* indicate more than one, yet the words *image* and *likeness* are singular. They are of the same species — God — yet their personalities and functions are completely different.

There are many verses in the Bible which show us the Holy Spirit's personality. For example, Paul tells us in Romans 8:27:

> **Now He who searches the hearts knows what the mind of the Spirit is, because He makes intercession for the saints according to the will of God.**

The word *Spirit* here is capitalized, as it should be. Usually, when you see *Spirit* capitalized, it refers to the Holy Spirit, not to man's spirit. You are a spirit. God is a Spirit. Jesus is a Spirit, angels are spirits, demons are spirits, Satan is a spirit, and the Holy Spirit is a Spirit.

The phrase *the mind of the Spirit* indicates the Holy Spirit has a mind. Having a mind presupposes having a will, and Paul adds in 1 Corinthians 12:11:

> But one and the same Spirit works all these
> things, distributing to each one individually as He
> wills.

So the Holy Spirit also has a will. In Isaiah 63:10, we have another aspect of the Holy Spirit listed:

> But they [the children of Israel] **rebelled and**
>   **grieved His Holy Spirit;**
> **So He turned Himself against them as an**
>   **enemy,**
> **And He fought against them.**

You have to have a personality to experience grief. According to this verse, the Holy Spirit can be grieved, so the Holy Spirit not only has a mind and a will, but also emotions.

We have still another aspect of the Holy Spirit shown to us in Genesis 6:3:

> **And the LORD said, "My Spirit shall not strive**
> **with man forever, for he is indeed flesh...."**

The statement *strive with man* does not mean we are engaged in a tug-of-war with the Holy Spirit. One of the purposes for the Holy Spirit's being here in the earth-realm is to awaken an awareness in unsaved people that they are estranged and separated from God, that God loves them, and that He has provided a way for their estrangement to be reconciled through Jesus Christ. He places that conviction in their hearts so they will seek God and eventually accept Jesus as their personal Savior and Lord. That is what is meant by the phrase *strive with man.*

Many ministers of the Gospel, especially many years ago, thought they were supposed to preach people under conviction. They would use everything they could to make people feel guilty so they could bring them to a place of accepting Christ as Savior and Lord. But that is not really the minister's job.

All the minister is supposed to do is impart the Word of God to the people. Faith comes by hearing the Word. Once that Word goes out, and faith comes, the Holy Spirit can bring an understanding to the individual hearing the Word that he or she needs Jesus as Savior and Lord.

Helper

Jesus reveals even more about the Holy Spirit in John 14:26:

> **"But the Helper, the Holy Spirit, whom the Father will send in My name, He will teach you all things, and bring to your remembrance all things that I said to you."**

The Holy Spirit teaches us, and He witnesses to us about the things of God. Jesus restates this in John 15:26, where He says:

"But when the Helper comes, whom I shall send to you from the Father, the Spirit of truth who proceeds from the Father, He will testify of Me."

In both these verses, Jesus uses the term *Helper*. That describes another job the Holy Spirit has — to assist or help the Body of Christ. The Holy Spirit is also the Spirit of truth. Whenever He is around, He will tell you only the truth. Whenever there are lies, the Holy Spirit is not involved.

Another duty assigned to the Holy Spirit is listed in John 16:8:

"And when He has come, He will convict the world of sin, and of righteousness, and of judgment."

The Holy Spirit will convict and convince the world — not the Church, but the world. This goes along with the *striving with man* that we saw in Genesis 6:3. The world needs to be convinced and convicted because it does not have the Word of God and needs Christ. The Church has the Word, and it should be brought under conviction relative to its relationship with the Lord by the Word.

Jesus adds in John 16:13:

"However, when He, the Spirit of truth, has come, He will guide you into all truth; for He will not speak on His own authority, but whatever He hears He will speak; and He will tell you things to come."

The Holy Spirit is the Christian's guide, and when He guides us, He will never lead us wrong. Many times, that is how you can know that a man and a women did not listen to the Holy Spirit before they got married. If the Holy Spirit had led them to believe it was okay for them to marry each other, they would never think of getting a divorce. If the couple ends up getting a divorce, that means the Holy Spirit did not know what He was doing when He led them to marry one another in the first place.

Now, I realize your will is also involved in making decisions as to whom you will marry, but the Holy Spirit will guide you. He will lead you into all truth. Some people have claimed that the Holy Spirit is an inanimate force that flows from God to move His people to do His bidding, but I cannot conceive of a force that would have the capacity to guide. Guiding involves giving directions and encouraging change. I cannot imagine any impersonal force having that kind of intelligence.

Paul tells us more about being guided by the Spirit in Romans 8:14. There he writes:

> **For as many as are led by the Spirit of God, these are sons of God.**

Does this mean that the people who are not led by the Spirit are not the sons of God? That is what Paul seems to imply here. But think about this: If the sons of God were led by the Spirit of God, it is obvious that the Spirit would not lead those people who are not sons of God. So why would you need to say anything?

Let me put it another way. In John 8:31-32, we have this statement:

> **Then Jesus said to those Jews who believed Him, "If you abide in My word, you are My disciples indeed.**
> **"And you shall know the truth, and the truth shall make you free."**

If is the qualifier here. Jesus says if we abide in His Word, we are His disciples indeed. But is Jesus also telling us that if we do not abide in the Word of God, we are not His disciples? In other words, is He telling us that we are not His disciples if we do not continue in the Word to the point that it is part of our lifestyle?

The answer to that question is no. If continuing in the Word were what made us disciples, that would disqualify Ephesians 2:8-9, which says, **For by grace you have been saved through faith, and that not of yourselves; it is the gift of God, not of works, lest anyone should boast.** Continuing in God's Word is a work. It is not a gift.

What Jesus means in John 8:31 is that if you continue in God's Word, you are the dedicated kind of disciple Jesus is looking for, and you will receive the benefits of being that kind of disciple. If you do not continue in God's Word, you will never fully know your covenant rights or privileges, and that will limit how much of the victorious life in Christ you are going to enjoy.

Likewise, in Romans 8:14, when Paul says, **For as many as are led by the Spirit of God, these are sons of God,** he is not saying that our salvation is predicated on our being led by the Spirit. What he is saying is that if we are truly sons of God, we will allow ourselves to be led by the Spirit. That should quicken you to ask yourself, "Am I being led by the Spirit?"

If you have to follow up that question with, "What is the Holy Spirit," then it is obvious you are not being led. Therefore, you will never enjoy your sonship with God to the fullest.

In the Comfort of the Spirit

Another aspect of the Holy Spirit is shown to us in Acts 9:31:

> **Then the churches throughout all Judea, Galilee, and Samaria had peace and were edified. And walking in the fear of the Lord and in the comfort of the Holy Spirit, they were multiplied.**

The Holy Spirit is in the earth-realm to comfort us. In fact, one of the names used in the original King James Bible to describe the Holy Spirit is the Comforter. He also reveals things to us, as Paul points out in 1 Corinthians 2:9-10:

But as it is written:

"Eye has not seen, nor ear heard,
Nor have entered into the heart of man
The things which God has prepared for those
    who love Him."

But God has revealed them to us through His Spirit. For the Spirit searches all things, yes, the deep things of God.

I read 1 Corinthians 2:9 for many years before I came into a knowledge of the Word. I would preach on that verse, and I heard other ministers preach on it — "Yes, but it is written, 'Eye has not seen, nor ear heard, nor have entered into the heart of man the things which God has prepared for those who love Him.' Hallelujah!" The congregation would shout, holler, and get emotional, but nobody would know after the sermon ended what God had prepared. We thought it was a mystery, and yet nobody ever noticed that Paul said in 1 Corinthians 2:10, **But God has revealed them.** *Has* means it is already done — and God has done it through His Spirit. The Holy Spirit is the one who reveals the deep things of God to us.

The reason we need to know about the deep things of God is that the deeper we go in the things of God, the higher we will go in victorious living. When building a skyscraper 100 stories high, the builders first have to dig down deep to lay the foundation. The taller the building, the further down the foundation has to go to support that building. The same is true with the things of God. If you want to go high in the things of God, you first have to go into the deep truths of His Word. You cannot do that without the Holy Spirit.

The Holy Spirit also sanctifies. Paul points out in Romans 15:16:

> that I might be a minister of Jesus Christ to the Gentiles, ministering the gospel of God, that the offering of the Gentiles might be acceptable, sanctified by the Holy Spirit.

Sanctify simply means "to set apart for holy service." Some people hear or read the word *sanctify*, and they think it means something especially holy. But that is not what it means at all. In its simplest definition, sanctify means "to set apart," and it is the Holy Spirit who does it.

Something else the Holy Spirit does is revealed to us in Romans 8:16:

> The Spirit Himself bears witness with our spirit that we are children of God.

The Holy Spirit witnesses to our spirit that we are the children of God. That is something you have to know spiritually — and by "spiritually," I do not mean emotionally. I do not mean to offend by my next statement, but I say it only to point out a fact. Especially for those of us who are in Black communities and in Black churches, we have been conditioned since the days of slavery to equate spirituality with emotionalism. If you are not careful, you will think you are being spiritual when you are actually being emotional.

Emotions are real, they are fine, and they are wonderful. You want to use your emotions when your team has just run 98 yards to make a touchdown, or when you are watching television or a movie and the good guys are overtaking the bad guys. But when it comes to the things of God, you really do not want your emotions to get in the way. It is alright if your emotions follow you into the things of God, but if you make the mistake of allowing yourself to be led or guided by your emotions, you will be tripped up every time. God is not an emotion. He is a Spirit, and you have to relate to God spiritually, not emotionally.

That is one reason walking by faith is so important. Your feelings are like the weather. You can feel emotionally high one minute and down in the dumps the next. Everything in the environment can affect your feelings, and once you let your feelings take over, you may not hear what the Spirit of God is saying to you. However, when you learn to walk by faith, by the Spirit, nothing in the environment will affect you, and you can pay closer attention to what the Holy Spirit is saying.

The Holy Spirit will not only witness to you, but He will also command you or forbid you from making a mistake. In Acts 16:6-7, we have this incident:

> **Now when they had gone through Phrygia
> and the region of Galatia, they were forbidden by
> the Holy Spirit to preach the word in Asia.**
> **After they had come to Mysia, they tried to go
> into Bithynia, but the Spirit did not permit them.**

Something like that happened to me many years ago. We were seeking financing for a 23-acre piece of property in order to expand the ministry, and we got into a situation with some people who were supposedly financiers. We did everything we could to check those people out. Their company checked out with Dunn and Bradstreet, and when your company checks out with Dunn and Bradstreet, it is supposed to be legitimate.

We met with these people, and they told us that in order to get the money we needed, we had to put some money up-front. We did not know at the time that no legitimate financial organization will require you to do that, because the company will get its money out of escrow anyway. A bank or other lending institution may want to charge a small amount of money as an application fee, but when people who supposedly work for a lending institution talk about charging several thousand dollars or more, you are dealing with crooks.

The people said they needed $210,000 from the church to consolidate the loan. Technically, they said, we could think of it as a down-payment on the loan, but we would get that money back when the loan went through. It sounded legitimate, and I went away from the meeting thinking, "Praise God, this seems like it is the way we should go." I went back to the church, and the church board voted to give these people the money.

I met for lunch with two of the people — supposedly one of the financiers and his secretary — not long afterwards, and I will never forget that meeting. I had brought a certified check for $210,000, and right after I handed the man the check, something went off inside of me. It was like there were bugs crawling inside me, gnawing away, and something told me, "This is not right." When the people left, I immediately telephoned the church's finance office. I told the person in charge there to call the bank right away to put a stop-payment on the check.

The people I gave the check to were supposed to take it to their headquarters in another state. However, thirty minutes after our meeting ended, they were in the bank where the church had its account. They were trying to get that check cashed into so many $100 bills, so many $50's, and so on. The bank would not cash the check, and we never heard from those "financiers" again.

The Holy Spirit will warn you about a situation that is not right, and He will protect you. That is another reason you need His ministry and help today. What you have to do is be sensitive enough, spiritually speaking, to listen to Him, and to have enough sense to trust Him.

Sometimes the Holy Spirit may speak to you directly. He may tell you through a dream. He may speak to you through another person, and you know the person talking has no knowledge of the situation, so his speaking about it has to be supernatural. Or the Holy Spirit may give you a prompting, like the feeling that a bunch of creatures are crawling around inside of you. But however the Holy Spirit warns you, thank God for it.

2

The Person of the Holy Spirit — Part 2

So far, we have learned that the Holy Spirit has a mind, a will, and emotions. We have learned that He strives, teaches, testifies, convicts, guides, comforts, helps, searches, reveals, sanctifies and commands. These characteristics are what we can call the personality of the Holy Spirit.

What we want to look at now is the fact that the Holy Spirit is susceptible to personal treatment. For instance, the Holy Spirit can be lied to. In Acts 5:1-4, we are told the following:

> But a certain man named Ananias, with Sapphira his wife, sold a possession.
> And he kept back part of the proceeds, his wife also being aware of it, and brought a certain part and laid it at the apostles' feet.
> But Peter said, "Ananias, why has Satan filled your heart to lie to the Holy Spirit and to keep back part of the price of the land for yourself?

> "While it remained, was it not your own? And after it was sold, was it not in your own control? Why have you conceived this thing in your heart? You have not lied to men but to God."

Not only can you lie to the Holy Spirit, but according to what Peter says here, when you lie to the Holy Spirit, you lie to God. As we learned in the previous chapter, the Holy Spirit is not God the Father, but He is still God.

You can also resist the Holy Spirit, according to Acts 7:51. There, Stephen told the people:

> "You stiff-necked and uncircumcised in heart and ears! You always resist the Holy Spirit; as your fathers did, so do you."

Still another thing you can do is blaspheme against the Holy Spirit. In Matthew 12:31-32, Jesus says:

> "Therefore I say to you, every sin and blasphemy will be forgiven men, but the blasphemy against the Spirit will not be forgiven men.
> "Anyone who speaks a word against the Son of Man, it will be forgiven him; but whoever speaks against the Holy Spirit, it will not be forgiven him, either in this age or in the age to come."

That sounds pretty heavy, but what does it really mean to blaspheme against the Holy Spirit? A simple definition would be "to deny, renounce or reject the Holy Spirit's testimony concerning Jesus as Savior and Lord."

In other words, if the Holy Spirit witnesses to a person's spirit that Jesus Christ is Savior and Lord, and that person says, "I don't believe that. I do not accept it," there is no way for that person to be forgiven *because he has rejected the only way to be forgiven, which is Jesus Christ.* How can that person get saved if he rejected the only way he can attain salvation? He cannot.

A scripture that illustrates this idea more clearly is Acts 4:12. There Peter says:

> **"Nor is there salvation in any other, for there is no other name under heaven given among men by which we must be saved."**

If you read the context of this verse, you will find that Peter is talking about Jesus. There is no option here. There is no debate. If you want to be saved, you have to do it through Jesus. That is an imperative necessity. Peter did not say, "... may." He said, **"... must."**

Some people get upset about that and say, "That's what I say about that Christianity stuff. Christians always try to put people in bondage. They are always trying to put them on a guilt trip." No — we are only trying to warn folks. If we all had 10,000 years to make our decision, I would say, "Take your time." But none of us know what is going to happen tomorrow. People can be here today and gone tomorrow, or here today and gone today. So there are really no second chances when it comes to becoming a Christian. It is do or die, now or never.

Do Not Grieve

Another thing you can do to the Holy Spirit is grieve Him. In Ephesians 4:30, Paul tells us:

And do not grieve the Holy Spirit of God, by whom you were sealed for the day of redemption.

If we are instructed not to grieve the Holy Spirit, that means He can be grieved. You might think, "How can I grieve the Holy Spirit?" The best way to answer that question is to reason from the known to the unknown. In other words, start out with what you know, and that will help you move on to what you do not know.

What causes you grief? What brings grief to you probably also brings grief to the Holy Spirit. Doesn't it grieve you when someone does not take you at your word? You are telling someone to do something, and the person thinks you are lying about it. In fact, the person almost goes so far as to call you a liar. That can hurt.

When the Holy Spirit tells you things through the Word of God as well as supernaturally, and you do not believe Him, that can cause Him grief. So can doing something that is unholy when He is living inside you. When you give your word to someone and do not fulfill that word, that can also grieve the Holy Spirit.

Another scripture that is very similar to Ephesians 4:30 is 1 Thessalonians 5:19:

Do not quench the Spirit.

We sometimes use the term *quench my thirst.* When you get very thirsty, you need water; water quenches or puts out the thirst. Another illustration of quenching something is when you pour water on a fire, and the water puts out or extinguishes that fire.

The way we can quench the Spirit is by doing things and having attitudes that have the same effect as throwing a bucket of water on a fire. That is one of the reasons I have gotten on the congregation on Sundays for being late to church. When we come together in one place, we are considered by God as one entity. Anything one person does that is contrary to what the group is doing can hinder everyone else in the group.

It is like the old saying, "A chain is as strong as its weakest link." The total strength of a chain has to be measured by its weakest link because that is where it is going to break. When Christians meet as a corporate body, they are like a chain from a spiritual point of view. Whenever someone grieves or quenches the Holy Spirit, the whole chain is weakened by that one link.

Here is another way we can grieve and quench the Holy Spirit. I teach the Word for two purposes: (1) to influence people to make a decision for the things of God, and (2) to feed the sheep and feed the lambs. When I get to the end of the lesson and give the invitation for people to accept Jesus as their personal Savior and Lord, I am expecting some fruit from my labor, because the Bible says that God confirms His Word with signs following.

Unless someone in the congregation knows the person next to him or her personally, he really does not know whether or not that person is a Christian. That person could be a sinner and on his last point of hope in life. We get to the end of the lesson, I tell the people, "Every head bowed, every eye closed," and the person sitting next to the sinner gets up and walks out. You can bet the devil is right there to whisper in the sinner's ear, "You go, too. It's a good time for you to go. You won't be embarrassed, because you won't be the only one leaving."

Now I realize there are people who have to go to work on Sunday, or catch a plane, or go to the restroom. That is alright, because the Spirit of God knows those people's motives, and that will give the Holy Spirit the liberty of holding back the sinner so He can witness to him. But if the reason people leave the service early is not a legitimate one, the Holy Spirit cannot hold that sinner back to minister to him.

The things I mentioned are little things, but they give the devil and demons the advantage when situations arise. I am thoroughly convinced that God wants to do great things in our midst, but He cannot do them if our attitudes and decorum are not right.

Divine Qualities

Now let's look at some things that will show us what is called the deity or god-likeness of the Holy Spirit. In Hebrews 9:14, Paul says:

> how much more shall the blood of Christ, who through the eternal Spirit offered Himself without spot to God, cleanse your conscience from dead works to serve the living God?

Notice, in the middle of this verse, **... who through the eternal Spirit.** Eternal means "everlasting," and the only thing that is everlasting is God.

In Psalm 139:7-10, we have another characteristic of the Holy Spirit revealed:

> Where can I go from Your Spirit?
> Or where can I flee from Your presence?
> If I ascend into heaven, You are there;
> If I make my bed in hell, behold, You are there.
> If I take the wings of the morning,
> And dwell in the uttermost parts of the sea,
> Even there Your hand shall lead me,
> And Your right hand shall hold me.

What the Psalmist is saying, in essence, is, "Wherever I go, I cannot get away from God's Spirit." The technical word for this is *omnipresence.* Omni means "all-encompassing," and *omnipresence* means "to be present everywhere at the same time."

You may think, "How can God be everywhere at the same time?" I don't know, but by the same token, how can the air be everywhere at the same time? You cannot even see the air, but let it go out of here and watch what happens. Omnipresence is an attribute of God the Father, and it is also an attribute of the Holy Spirit.

Another verse that tells us something about the God-likeness of the Holy Spirit is 1 Corinthians 2:10:

> **But God has revealed them to us through His Spirit. For the Spirit searches all things, yes, the deep things of God.**

Here, we get into another one of these *omni's*. This one is called *omniscience*, which means "all-knowing." In order to search all things, the Holy Spirit would have to know all things, because He would have to know what and where to search. So the Holy Spirit, like God the Father, is omniscient.

The Holy Spirit is also credited with the ability to perform divine works. For instance, the Holy Spirit was involved in the creation of the world. In Genesis 1:1-3, we are told the following:

> **In the beginning God created the heavens and the earth.**
> **The earth was without form, and void; and darkness was on the face of the deep. And the Spirit of God was hovering over the face of the waters.**
> **Then God said, "Let there be light"; and there was light.**

The Holy Spirit is the third person in what is called the Godhead. The Godhead functions like a corporation. God the Father is president and chief executive officer. Jesus is executive vice president and director of operations. The Holy Spirit is the field representative. While Jesus and the Father stay and issue orders from corporate headquarters in heaven, the Holy Spirit goes into the earth-realm to carry out those orders.

As the Spirit of God hovered over the face of the waters and the Father God spoke, the Spirit of God caused what God spoke to come into being. Therefore, we could say that the Holy Spirit is the power source God used to create the world. The Holy Spirit is the power source of the Godhead. A way to illustrate this point would be to picture the Godhead as a car, and the Holy Spirit as the engine of that car.

Jesus tells us another area where the power of the Holy Spirit is used in John 3:5-6:

> **Jesus answered, "Most assuredly, I say to you, unless one is born of water and the Spirit, he cannot enter the kingdom of God.**
> **"That which is born of the flesh is flesh, and that which is born of the Spirit is spirit."**

Notice, in the sixth verse, the first time the word *Spirit* is used, it is capitalized. Whenever you see the word *Spirit* capitalized in the Bible, it is referring or should be referring to the Holy Spirit. The second time *spirit* is used in this verse, it is in lower case, because it is referring to the spirit of man. You do not have a spirit. You are a spirit. You have a soul, and you live in a physical body. We are made in the image and likeness of God, and God is a Spirit. Therefore, we — you and I — are also spirits.

I mentioned in chapter one that the Holy Spirit is the one who witnesses to unsaved people's hearts that they are estranged from God. The Holy Spirit is also the one who causes the new birth to take place. Medical science tells us that a man produces a sperm, a woman produces an egg, and that when a sperm and an egg come together in a woman's womb, all things being equal, conception takes place, and a child is the result. A sperm cannot come into contact with bone and produce a child. An egg cannot come into contact with a hair follicle and produce a child. So there is some unseen, unknown force that produces life as a result of the sperm and the egg coming together.

When the Holy Spirit and the Word of God, which is the actual seed of God, come together, fertilization takes place and a child is born out of the world into Christ Jesus. That is why Jesus says in John 3:5, **"... unless one is born of water and the Spirit, he cannot enter the kingdom of God."** It is the Holy Spirit who causes that birth to take place. It is also why Jesus adds in John 3:6:

> **"That which is born of the flesh is flesh, and that which is born of the Spirit is spirit."**

All that flesh can do is produce more flesh, and all the Spirit can do is produce more spirit. That is why there cannot be any such thing as evolution in terms of the whole human race coming from a one-celled creature that crept out of the primordial sea. That is impossible. We are told in Genesis 1:21:

> So God created great sea creatures and every living thing that moves, with which the waters abounded, according to their kind, and every winged bird according to its kind. And God saw that it was good.

Everything **abounded according to its kind** or **according to their kind.** Elephants did not develop from tigers, and tigers did not develop from dogs. Everything came completely developed from the hand of God. You can cross-breed dogs and get a little different variety of this or that dog, but you will never put two dogs together and produce a cat. What you get will still be a dog.

Raiser of the Dead

Another divine attribute that is ascribed to the Holy Spirit is the ability to raise the dead. Paul says in Romans 8:11:

> But if the Spirit of Him who raised Jesus from the dead dwells in you, He who raised Christ from the dead will also give life to your mortal bodies through His Spirit who dwells in you.

The Holy Spirit raised Jesus from the dead, and He will raise us from the dead if we physically die before Jesus returns.

One more divine attribute of the Holy Spirit is that He proceeds or comes from the heavenly Father. Jesus says in John 15:26:

> "But when the Helper comes, whom I shall send to you from the Father, the Spirit of truth who proceeds from the Father, He will testify of Me."

He continues in John 16:7 by saying:

> "Nevertheless I tell you the truth. It is to your advantage that I go away; for if I do not go away, the Helper will not come to you; but if I depart, I will send Him to you."

The Holy Spirit comes from the Father. He has been here for 2,000 years, and He is here now, ready to empower us, guide us, teach us and help us. He is ready to comfort us and stand by us in our time of need. All we have to do is allow Him to do so.

3

Terms and Misconceptions — Part 1

Before we go any further, I want to take time to give you some definitions and clarify some terminology. Many of the problems people have had with what we will discuss in the rest of this book is simply a case of misunderstanding. Too often, we go by some statement we heard in some church without any scriptural support to back up what was said. What we heard may have sounded clever, but from a biblical perspective, it is totally wrong.

For example, if you have been a Christian any length of time, you have probably heard the terms *being filled with the Spirit, baptized with the Spirit,* and *receiving the gift of the Spirit.* All three of these terms are used in the Bible to describe the same event. In Acts 2:4, we have this account:

> **And they were all filled with the Holy Spirit and began to speak with other tongues, as the Spirit gave them utterance.**

And in Acts 11:15-17, when Peter was explaining to the church fathers why he went to the house of a Gentile named Cornelius, he told them:

> **"And as I began to speak, the Holy Spirit fell upon them, as upon us at the beginning.**
>
> **"Then I remembered the word of the Lord, how He said, 'John indeed baptized with water, but you shall be baptized with the Holy Spirit.'**
>
> **"If therefore God gave them the same gift as He gave us...."**

Many Christians have wondered why the Bible gives us three terms to describe the same transaction. The reason there are three different terms is that there are three different people involved in the same transaction. On Jesus' side of the ledger, it is Jesus baptizing you with the Holy Spirit. On your side of the ledger, it is you receiving the gift of the Holy Spirit. And on the Holy Spirit's side of the transaction, it is the Holy Spirit infilling you.

Another point of confusion for many Christians has been the terms *the baptism of the Holy Spirit* and *the baptism with the Holy Spirit*. There is a baptism of the Holy Spirit, and there is a baptism with the Holy Spirit, and they are entirely different. Yet traditionally, those terms have been used to talk about the same thing.

Let me give you a little background of my personal experience with Jesus Christ, because my confusion over these two terms is typical of the dilemma many people experience. I was not brought up in the church, and did not accept Christ as my personal Savior and Lord until the year I was married. When I was saved, I was encouraged to associate myself with a local church, so I would have fellowship, as well as grow in the things of God. My wife, who accepted Christ at an early age, happened to be raised a Baptist, so we decided to attend a Baptist church in the area.

About a month after we started attending that church, the Lord called me into the ministry. I was in the church when Jesus spoke to me as He spoke to Paul on the Damascus road. He told me, in what seemed to me to be an audible voice, "You are to preach My Gospel." I heard it so clearly that I turned around to see who spoke to me. Nobody was there, so I knew it had to be Jesus, and that I had been called into the ministry.

After we had attended the church a while, I started hearing words like *sanctification, righteousness, Holy Spirit.* I had also begun reading the Bible, and I would read these accounts of people being filled with the Spirit. I asked the people at the church about being filled with the Spirit, and I was told that when I accepted Jesus as my personal Savior and Lord, I was automatically filled with the Holy Spirit.

I went on for 17 years thinking I was filled with the Holy Sprit. Eventually, I reached a point where I was spiritually dry. I knew there was something missing, but I did not know what that something was. I did not know how to explain it, where to find it, or what to do. I was so frustrated that I was ready to say, "Forget it," and leave the ministry. Finally, the Lord showed me through various situations that I was not filled with the Spirit.

It is scripturally impossible for you to accept Jesus Christ as your personal Savior and Lord and be filled at the same time. In other words, it is impossible for you to be born again at 12:00 and to be filled with the Spirit at 12:00. Jesus tells us in John 14:16-17:

> **"And I will pray the Father, and He will give you another Helper, that He may abide with you forever —**
>
> **"the Spirit of truth, whom the world cannot receive, because it neither sees Him nor knows Him...."**

The words *Helper* and *Spirit of truth* refer to the Holy Spirit. Jesus says in verse 17, **"the Spirit of truth, whom the world cannot receive."** Cannot means "not possible — it will not happen." Now notice what Jesus says in a very familiar verse of scripture — John 3:16:

> **"For God so loved the world that He gave His only begotten Son, that whoever believes in Him should not perish but have everlasting life."**

The world is another term for the sinner, and a sinner is a non-Christian — someone who is not in the family of God. If the world cannot receive the Spirit of truth, it means sinners cannot receive the Holy Spirit.

Let me ask you a question. What is a person when he or she accepts Jesus Christ as Savior and Lord? A sinner, because a sinner is the only person who needs to receive Him. If what they told me in the Baptist church I attended were true, and I had received the Holy Spirit at the same time I was saved, that would mean I received the Holy Spirit while I was still a sinner. From what we just read in John, that is biblically impossible.

It is entirely possible to be saved and live your whole life without being filled with the Spirit. In the eighth chapter of Acts, starting at verse 14, we read the following:

> **Now when the apostles who were at Jerusalem heard that Samaria had received the word of God** [in other words, that the people had received Jesus], **they sent Peter and John to them.**

If the apostles in Jerusalem sent Peter and John to the Samaritans who had heard and received the Word, they must have sent them for a purpose. That purpose is spelled out in the next verse.

> **who, when they had come down, prayed for them that they might receive the Holy Spirit.**

Since Peter and John were sent to pray for the people to receive the Holy Spirit, receiving must not be automatic. Otherwise, why would the apostles have wasted their time, the Samaritans' time, and Peter and John's time by sending Peter and John to pray for the people?

Read Acts 8:15 once more, and notice something else.

> who, when they had come down, prayed for them that they might receive....

It does not say that Peter and John prayed that the people *would* receive, but that the people *might* receive. You can refuse to be filled with the Holy Spirit, and people in many churches have done so. If the infilling with the Holy Spirit were automatic, this verse would not say anything about the people's responsibility in the matter.

Acts 8:16:

> For as yet He had fallen upon none of them. They had only been baptized in the name of the Lord Jesus.

Make a special note of the word *only*. These people had been baptized in the name of Jesus. They were Believers, yet they were not filled with the Holy Spirit.

Acts 8:17:

> Then they [Peter and John] laid hands on them, and they received the Holy Spirit.

The Holy Spirit did not suddenly come upon the people, or force Himself upon them, when Peter and John laid hands on them. It says they *received* Him — and *received* indicates a willful act on the part of the receiver.

Your salvation does not hinge upon being filled with the Spirit. You should be filled, and we will find out why a little later in this book, but it has nothing to do with whether or not you go to heaven when you physically die. Paul tells us in Romans 10:9:

> that if you confess with your mouth the Lord Jesus and believe in your heart that God has raised Him from the dead, you will be saved.

The two prerequisites for your salvation are believing in your heart and confessing with your mouth. Being filled with the Spirit is not even mentioned. Not only does Paul not mention it, but notice a statement Jesus makes in Mark 16:15-16:

> And He said to them, "Go into all the world and preach the gospel to every creature.
> "He who believes and is baptized will be saved; but he who does not believe will be condemned."

The Holy Spirit is not mentioned here, either. Jesus does not say, "He who believes and is filled with the Spirit will be saved."

Three Baptisms

Now let me drop a real cobalt bomb on some of you. Believe it or not, the Bible speaks of three different baptisms that every child of God should go through. Each of these baptisms is different and has a different purpose. Most people in mainline denominational churches find out about only one of these baptisms, but every Christian needs to go through the other two baptisms, as well.

In Hebrews 6:1, Paul tells us:

> **Therefore, leaving the discussion of the elementary principles of Christ....**

Paul is not talking about the elementary principles of Crenshaw Christian Center, or the elementary principles of Frederick K.C. Price. He is talking about the elementary principles of Christ. And since Jesus is the same yesterday, today, and forever, His principles do not change. Whatever they were, they are and will continue to be.

> **Therefore, leaving the discussion of the elementary principles of Christ, let us go on to perfection....**

Perfection does not mean flawlessness. It is wonderful if you can attain to flawlessness, and you will be in better shape for doing so. But *perfection* here literally means "maturity" — in other words, to grow up.

Another word for *elementary principles* is *fundamentals,* and another word for *fundamentals* is *basics.* You usually do not start out in mathematics by studying calculus or trigonometry. You usually start out with addition and subtraction. Those are the basics. When you advance to calculus and trigonometry, you are going into more mature types of mathematics.

Paul is telling us that we should get away from the basics of Christ and move on to maturity. It is the basics that give us the foundation for growing into maturity. Unfortunately, so many Christians do not even know the basics yet! They may have been saved 25, 35, 40 years or more, and they are still spiritual babies — babies in their knowledge of the Word of God.

A lot of people want to have something different every week, and the minister goes on to the 25th new sermon when the people have not mastered what he taught in his first sermon. We need to stay "in first grade" until we learn what we need to know. Then we can go on to the next level.

Paul goes on in Hebrews 6:1-2 by saying:

> ... let us go on to perfection, not laying again the foundation of repentance from dead works and of faith toward God [this is talking about repentance], of the doctrine of baptisms....

Notice that the word *baptism* has an *s* on it. That implies plurality, and plurality means more than one. I am not talking about advanced studies, or about special doctrinal programs. I am talking about fundamentals — basics — and baptisms are included in the fundamentals.

... of laying on of hands....

Think about it — the laying on of hands is a fundamental doctrine of Jesus Christ. In all the years I spent in the Baptist, Methodist and Presbyterian churches, the only time they laid hands on people was when they were ordaining someone to the ministry. They never laid hands on the sick, and we had a lot of sick people.

... of resurrection of the dead....

Notice what Paul did not say. He did not say, "... of *the* resurrection of the dead." The reason Paul says **of resurrection** is that there will be two resurrections — the resurrection of the just and the resurrection of the unjust. The people who take part in the resurrection of the just are going to be in the Kingdom of God, but the people in the resurrection of the unjust will go to the Lake of Fire.

... and of eternal judgment.

Again, Paul does not say "and of the eternal judgment." He says **of eternal judgment** because there is going to be more than one.

As I mentioned earlier, there are three baptisms every Christian should go through. Before I talk about these baptisms in more detail, I want to go back to the very beginning of the subject of baptism. If we do not understand what baptism itself means, we will never understand what any of the three baptisms really means, either.

In Luke 20:1-4, we have the following:

> Now it happened on one of those days, as He taught the people in the temple and preached the gospel, that the chief priests and the scribes, together with the elders, confronted Him
>
> and spoke to Him, saying, "Tell us, by what authority are You doing these things? Or who is he who gave You this authority?"
>
> But He answered and said to them, "I also will ask you one thing, and answer Me:
>
> "The baptism of John [that is, John the Baptist] — was it from heaven or from men?"

Let me ask you the question Jesus posed: Was the baptism of John from heaven, or from the local church? Simple question, simple answer — it came from heaven. Because the baptism of John is from heaven, we have to find out heaven's definition of it. Since baptism did not come from man, man cannot say what baptism is.

The word *baptism* comes from the Greek word *baptizo*, which means "to dip into, immerse, or submerge." When you submerge something in water, you completely cover that object with water.

Some churches will sprinkle you and call it baptism, but does that practice come from heaven, or from the local church? We have no record in the

Bible where they said, "In the name of the Father, of the Son, and of the Holy Spirit," and sprinkled water on the person. We have no place in the Bible that says that John took a pitcher of water, poured the water over the person's head, and said, "In the name of the Father, of the Son, and of the Holy Spirit, I baptize you in water."

Also consider this: If I were to dip my fingers into some water and put my wet fingers on a person's head, or if I took a cup of water and poured it onto a person's head, it would not take much water to baptize that person. In fact, if you just sprinkled a person, you could probably baptize 5,000 people and not use more than a gallon of water.

Keep that thought in mind and read John 3:22-23:

> **After these things Jesus and His disciples came into the land of Judea, and there He remained with them and baptized.**
> **Now John also was baptizing in Aenon near Salim, because there was much water there. And they came and were baptized.**

Why would the Holy Spirit have John write **much water** in verse 23? Why not just say "water"? Because you need much water when you immerse people. You need a lot of water because the people's clothing will soak up some of the water and take it away from the pool; and if you baptize 5,000 people, the people are going to take away a whole lot of water with them.

Remember the term **much water** and read Matthew 3:13-16:

> **Then Jesus came from Galilee to John at the Jordan to be baptized by him.**
>
> **And John tried to prevent Him, saying, "I need to be baptized by You, and You are coming to me?"**
>
> **But Jesus answered and said to him, "Permit it to be so now, for thus it is fitting for us to fulfill all righteousness." Then he allowed Him.**
>
> **When He had been baptized, Jesus came up immediately from the water....**

You do not come up unless you have been down, so Jesus must have been down in the water, not standing someplace where someone was sprinkling water on people. *Up* indicates that John the Immerser had put Jesus under the water, which would correspond to the definition of *baptizo* — to immerse, dip into or submerge.

Two Ministries

John the Baptist indicated that Jesus would have two distinct ministries. In John 1:29, we have this statement:

> **The next day John saw Jesus coming toward him, and said, "Behold! The Lamb of God who takes away the sin of the world!"**

That was Jesus' first ministry, His first and primary purpose — to become the Lamb of God to take away the sin of the world. Notice, John did not say, "Behold! The Lamb of God who takes away the s-i-n-s of the world!" Jesus did not come to take away the s-i-n-s of the world. He came to take away the sin of the world, because if you get rid of the sin, you will not have any problem with the sins. Sins are symptomatic; they are the result of something that causes them to manifest. Sin is causative. If you change the cause, you will change the effect, and Jesus came to deal with the cause.

Jesus' second ministry is also mentioned in the first chapter of John, this time in verse 33. John the Baptist is still speaking, and he says:

> **"I did not know Him, but He who sent me to baptize with water said to me, 'Upon whom you see the Spirit descending, and remaining on Him, this is He who baptizes with the Holy Spirit.'"**

John the Baptist used water to baptize people, so the element John put people into was water. According to what John the Baptist says here, Jesus was going to baptize people with the Holy Spirit, so the element Jesus was going to use was the Holy Spirit. That is Jesus' second ministry — to baptize people with the Holy Spirit.

Paul writes in Hebrews 13:8:

> **Jesus Christ is the same yesterday, today, and forever.**

If Jesus does not baptize with the Holy Spirit today, this scripture is invalid. It would have to say that Jesus used to be the same, but He is not the same anymore. Jesus still takes away sin, and if He takes away sin, He must still baptize with the Holy Spirit.

The First Baptism

Let us go on to talk about the first of the three baptisms — the baptism of the Holy Spirit. Actually, every Christian has already experienced it, and most of them do not know it. Every Christian has to experience the baptism of the Holy Spirit, because if you do not experience it, you are not saved. Paul tells us in 1 Corinthians 12:12-13:

> For as the body is one and has many members, but all the members of that one body, being many, are one body, so also is Christ.
> For by one Spirit we were all baptized into one body — whether Jews or Greeks, whether slaves or free — and have all been made to drink into one Spirit.

Paul says, **For by one Spirit.** That means the Holy Spirit baptizes us into the Body of Christ. Imagine a swimming pool full of water. Someone pushes you into the pool and you sink to the bottom. If someone at the edge of the pool were to look at the water's level, he would not see you. The surface of the water would be flat, because you are under the water. You have actually become a part of the water, because to the other person's eye, the water is the same as it was before you went in.

The Holy Spirit takes us and "pushes us into the pool" of the Body of Christ, and we become an integral part of the Body. The Holy Spirit is the one who does this; that is why it is called the baptism of the Holy Spirit.

One Lord, One Faith, One Baptism?

Now go to Ephesians 4:1-6, and I will show you an apparent contradiction to the idea of more than one baptism. This is how the uninformed reader of the Bible can read the Word and think it contradicts itself:

> **I, therefore, the prisoner of the Lord, beseech you to walk worthy of the calling with which you were called,**
> **with all lowliness and gentleness, with long-suffering, bearing with one another in love,**
> **endeavoring to keep the unity of the Spirit in the bond of peace.**
> **There is one body and one Spirit, just as you were called in one hope of your calling;**
> **one Lord, one faith, one baptism;**
> **one God and Father of all, who is above all, and through all, and in you all.**

We read in Hebrews about baptisms, plural, and here Paul says **one baptism.** How do you reconcile that? Go back to verse one and I will show you how this segment of scripture goes right along with what we just read in 1 Corinthians 12:13. Paul is actually talking about salvation in Ephesians 4, and if you follow along, you will be able to see this very clearly. In verse one, Paul starts by saying:

> I, therefore, the prisoner of the Lord, beseech you to walk worthy of the calling with which you were called.

Every man is called to become a son of God.

Ephesians 4:2-4:

> with all lowliness and gentleness, with long-suffering, bearing with one another in love,
> endeavoring to keep the unity of the Spirit in the bond of peace.
> There is one body and one Spirit, just as you were called in one hope of your calling.

We read in 1 Corinthians 12:13 how we were all baptized into one body by one Spirit. Paul is saying the same thing in Ephesians 4:4. Then he adds in Ephesians 4:5:

> one Lord, one faith....

That is faith in the shed blood and resurrection of Christ.

> **one Lord** [the Lord Jesus Christ], **one faith** [faith in the shed blood of Christ and the resurrection], **one baptism** [the baptism of the Holy Spirit].

The baptism of the Holy Spirit is the only baptism that will save you. That is what Jesus was talking about in John 3:6 when He said, **"That which is born of the flesh is flesh, and that which is born of the Spirit is spirit."** The Holy Spirit recreates a man's spirit and places that man into the Body of Christ. The only way that can take place is by the baptism of the Holy Spirit. Water baptism will not do it, and neither will the baptism *with* the Holy Spirit.

4

Terms and Misconceptions — Part 2

Let us go on to the second of the three baptisms — water baptism. Actually, the second and third baptisms can be switched around, because it does not matter which one you participate in second, or which one you participate in third. You must be baptized into the Body of Christ first — that is a must. But when it comes to being baptized in water or being baptized with the Holy Spirit, either one can come before the other. There is no divine order.

In the second chapter of Acts, there is a scripture some denominations swear by when it comes to which order these baptisms are done. In verse 38, Peter addresses the crowd that formed after the 120 disciples in the upper room were filled with the Holy Spirit, and we have this statement:

> Then Peter said to them, "Repent, and let every one of you be baptized in the name of Jesus Christ for the remission of sins; and you shall receive the gift of the Holy Spirit."

Some people take that chronology — repent, be baptized in water, then receive the gift of the Holy Spirit — and become fixated on it to the point that they believe you always have to repent first, be baptized in water second, and receive the gift of the Holy Spirit third. Some of these people even teach that if you do not do those things in that order, you cannot become filled with the Spirit.

Who would know better than anyone else whether or not Peter's statement in Acts 2:38 is actually a statement of divine order? It would be Jesus, the head of the Church, God the Father, and the Holy Spirit. So if what Peter said were a statement of divine order, we would see that order in every case recorded in the Bible in which people accepted Christ. In every instance, it would be (1) saved, (2) water baptism, and (3) filled with the Holy Spirit, with no exceptions.

Acts 8:14-16:

> **Now when the apostles who were at Jerusalem heard that Samaria had received the word of God, they sent Peter and John to them,**
> **who, when they had come down, prayed for them that they might receive the Holy Spirit.**
> **For as yet He had fallen upon none of them. They had only been baptized in the name of the Lord Jesus.**

That follows the same order we read in Acts 2:38.

Acts 10:44-47:

> While Peter was still speaking these words, the Holy Spirit fell upon all those who heard the word.
> And those of the circumcision who believed were astonished, as many as came with Peter, because the gift of the Holy Spirit had been poured out on the Gentiles also.
> For they heard them speak with tongues and magnify God. Then Peter answered,
> "Can anyone forbid water, that these should not be baptized who have received the Holy Spirit just as we have?"

Here is a case where number one was repent, but number two was not water baptism. Number two in this case was the baptism with the Holy Spirit, and number three was water baptism. Apparently, it does not matter to the heavenly Father, Jesus, or the Holy Spirit whether or not you are baptized in water before you are filled with the Holy Spirit.

Another point where people become confused is that they think you cannot be saved unless you are baptized in water. In Mark 16:15-16, Jesus says this:

> And He said to them, "Go into all the world and preach the gospel to every creature.
> "He who believes and is baptized will be saved...."

It looks as though Jesus is saying you have to be baptized in water to be saved, and I would agree with that if Jesus had stopped right there. But that is not the end of the thought. He goes on to say:

> **"... but he who does not believe will be condemned."**

If being baptized in water were absolutely essential, the latter part of this verse would have to read, "... but he who does not believe and is not baptized will be condemned." Jesus says the condemnation comes from not believing, not from not being baptized.

Water baptism for the Christian is like a wedding ring for a married person. In our society, a ring worn on the third finger of the left hand indicates that you are married. The ring does not marry you; it is simply a sign or a symbol of the fact that you are married. A married person could take the ring off his or her hand, and that person would still be just as married as he or she was with the ring on.

Paul tells us in Romans 7:1-4:

> **Or do you not know, brethren (for I speak to those who know the law), that the law has dominion over a man as long as he lives?**
>
> **For the woman who has a husband is bound by the law to her husband as long as he lives. But if the husband dies, she is released from the law of her husband.**
>
> **So then if, while her husband lives, she marries another man, she will be called an adulteress;**

but if her husband dies, she is free from that law, so that she is no adulteress, though she has married another man.

Therefore, my brethren, you also have become dead to the law through the body of Christ, that you may be married to another — to Him who was raised from the dead, that we should bear fruit to God.

We are married to Jesus, we have a wedding ring, and that ring is water baptism. That is all water baptism really is. It does not marry you to Jesus. It is a mark of identification — it identifies you with Jesus, and says that you belong to Him.

You should be baptized in water so that you can let everyone know you are married to Jesus. Personally, I think something is wrong with a married person who does not want to wear a wedding ring. Is that person ashamed of his wife or her husband? What is that person's problem?

Another way we are identified with Christ through water baptism is mentioned in Romans 6:1-5:

What shall we say then? Shall we continue in sin that grace may abound?

Certainly not! How shall we who died to sin live any longer in it?

Or do you not know that as many of us as were baptized into Christ Jesus were baptized into His death?

Therefore we were buried with Him through baptism into death, that just as Christ was raised from the dead by the glory of the Father, even so we also should walk in newness of life.

> **For if we have been united together in the likeness of His death, certainly we also shall be in the likeness of His resurrection.**

Not only does water baptism identify us as being married to Christ, but it also identifies us with Him in His death, burial, and resurrection. That is one more reason the only form of baptism that could approximate what the Bible says is the purpose of baptism is immersion.

We do not take a dead body, put it on the ground, and call that a burial. Neither do we put a dead body on the ground, sprinkle or pour a bagful of dirt on it, and call that a burial. When we bury a body, we totally enclose or encase it in something. We may place it in a mausoleum, a crypt, a pyramid, or a hole in the ground, but in any case, the body is totally covered from the outside world.

That is what happens when we go underwater, and that is why immersion is the only type of water baptism in which we can be identified with Christ in His burial and resurrection. It is the only way you can fulfill the symbolism water baptism is supposed to represent.

Another point of confusion regarding water baptism is that some churches believe if you do not baptize someone in Jesus' name, the person is not baptized. Other churches believe you have to baptize in the name of the Lord Jesus Christ. Some people believe you have to baptize in the name of the Lord, and others believe that if you do not baptize in the name of the Father, the Son, and the Holy Spirit, a person is not baptized. Who is right? They can't all be right, because that would be confusion.

It is the water which baptizes a person. All the things that we say and all the other methods people use is not what baptizes anyone. If we do not get the person into the water, the person is not baptized, so it does not make any difference what we say. In Matthew 28:19, Jesus says:

> "Go therefore and make disciples of all the nations, baptizing in the name of the Father and of the Son and of the Holy Spirit."

This is the head of the Church talking, who bought and paid for the Church with His blood. But notice what is conspicuous in its absence. Jesus tells us, **"Go ... baptizing in the name of the Father and of the Son and of the Holy Spirit."** There is no *s* on the end of the word *name*. Yet *Father, Son, and Holy Spirit* is plural, because it indicates three different individuals. Since Jesus does not say "names," He must be trying to tell us something.

Jesus is trying to tell us that the name of the Father, the Son, and the Holy Spirit in the earth-realm is the name of Jesus. That is the representative name of the Godhead in the earth. When you say the name of Jesus, you have the Father, the Son, the Holy Spirit, and all the resources of heaven behind that name.

Now I know from experience that some people will read the last few pages and, if they are not careful, they will get under condemnation and ask themselves, "Was I really baptized?" Some of these people were baptized in the name of the Lord. Some of them were baptized in the name of the Father, the Son, and the Holy Spirit. Some of these people were baptized by having water sprinkled on them. Some were baptized by having water poured on them, and some were baptized by immersion.

If you ask yourself, "Was I really baptized," here is how you can answer the question. I have told you what baptism means. You decide whether or not you were symbolically buried and resurrected with Christ when you were baptized in water. Do not get in bondage about it, because water baptism does not save you, anyway. But if you have a problem with how you were baptized, you should do what you need to do to fix the problem.

The Baptism With the Holy Spirit

A new Believer is placed in the Body of Christ by the Holy Spirit. He is baptized in water by the visible church. Now that Believer needs to be baptized with the Holy Spirit, so he can be energized and supernaturally empowered to live the born-again life the way God wants it lived. We have too many people who want to live the Christian life according to their own rules and regulations, and living the Christian life does not work that way. We have to do it according to the rule book, and the Bible is the rule book.

God tells us through the mouth of the prophet in Ezekiel 36:26-27:

> "I will give you a new heart and put a new spirit within you; I will take the heart of stone out of your flesh and give you a heart of flesh.
> "I will put My Spirit within you and cause you to walk in My statutes, and you will keep My judgments and do them."

God is not talking in verse 26 about the organ that pumps blood through your body. If He took that out of your flesh, you would be in trouble. He is talking symbolically about the heart or the spirit of man. You were given a brand new spirit when you were born again. That is what Paul means in 2 Corinthians 5:17 when he tells us:

> Therefore, if anyone is in Christ, he is a new creation; old things have passed away; behold, all things have become new.

However, the only old things that are passed away are the things in the spirit part of our nature. Not in our flesh, nor in our soul — just in our spirit. We need supernatural help for us to overcome the traditions and garbage we may have in our minds. It is a constant battle, because our minds and bodies will pull on us to do what they want to do. That is one reason we need the power of the Holy Spirit — to help our recreated human spirits do God's will and follow His Word.

Jesus gives us another reason in Acts 1:8:

> "But you shall receive power when the
> Holy Spirit has come upon you; and you shall
> be witnesses to Me in Jerusalem, and in all Judea
> and Samaria, and to the end of the earth."

When indicates that before the time *when* occurs, you do not have whatever it is *when* is referring to. Jesus told the disciples to stay in Jerusalem until the Holy Spirit came upon them, and they received power. Once they received that power, they would be witnesses of and for Him in Jerusalem, and in all Judea and Samaria, and to the end of the earth.

"To the end of the earth" actually refers to us. The disciples did not know about a North American continent, or a South American continent, or the islands of the sea, because they lived all their lives in a small area, geographically speaking. Jesus had to be talking about all the people who would believe in Him as an eventual result of the disciples' ministry. This includes us.

There are too many cases of a lot of zeal and commitment being expelled without any power, and a direct result of that is a lot of mediocre witnessing. Jesus would not tell us about receiving the power if we did not need it. And when it comes to going about the Lord's business, we definitely need it. The word translated as *power* in Acts 1:8 really means "ability." Without the power of the Holy Spirit, we do not have the supernatural ability to be as effective as we can be.

We need to be witnesses on Jesus' terms, because Paul tells us in 1 Corinthians 3:9:

For we are God's fellow workers; you are God's field, you are God's building.

He adds in 2 Corinthians 6:1:

We then, as workers together with Him also plead with you not to receive the grace of God in vain.

We are not workers *for* God; we are workers *with* Him. That is a very important distinction. It implies that God is doing something, and He is privileging us to assist Him. However, you cannot be a worker with God without His power.

That makes it vitally important for us to not only find out what our assignment from God is, but also to get ahold of His power so we can fulfill that task. That is why we need to be filled with the Holy Spirit — so we can operate in the same power and ability that God operates in.

For Every Believer?

Something else I would like you to keep in mind is that Paul wrote the books of 1 and 2 Corinthians to the family of God, not to the world. He was writing to every person in the family of God — male, female, the young, the old, everyone — because every person in the Body of Christ is a worker together with God.

Sometimes Christians have the idea that unless you are called by God to be an apostle, prophet, evangelist, pastor or teacher, you do not need the power of the Holy Spirit. But we all need it. All born-again Believers need the power so they can be witnesses to the world of the reality of Jesus Christ as Savior and Lord.

A scripture that shows us that being filled with the Holy Spirit is for every Believer is John 7:37-39:

> **On the last day, that great day of the feast, Jesus stood and cried out, saying, "If anyone thirsts, let him come to Me and drink.**
>
> **"He who believes in Me, as the Scripture has said, out of his heart will flow rivers of living water."**
>
> **But this He spoke concerning the Spirit, whom those believing in Him would receive; for the Holy Spirit was not yet given, because Jesus was not yet glorified.**

In the original King James, John 7:39 is more accurately translated, **(But this spake he of the Spirit, which they that believe on him should receive).** As I mentioned earlier in this book, being filled with the Spirit is not automatic. It is a gift you decide to receive. But no matter who you are in the Body of Christ, you can be filled.

Another scripture that backs this up is Acts 2:38-39:

> **Then Peter said to them, "Repent, and let every one of you be baptized in the name of Jesus Christ for the remission of sins; and you shall receive the gift of the Holy Spirit.**

> "For the promise is to you and to your children,
> and to all who are afar off, as many as the Lord our
> God will call."

Let me ask you this question: Has God called anyone into the family of God other than apostles, prophets, evangelists, pastors and teachers? Of course He has. Keep that in mind and read verse 39 again.

> "For the promise is to you...."

You refers to the people Peter was talking to on the day of Pentecost.

> "For the promise is to you and to your children,
> and to all who are afar off, as many as the Lord our
> God will call."

Will call includes us. Is God calling anyone into the family of God today? Yes! Then the promise Peter mentions is for every person in the Body of Christ today.

Peter adds in 2 Peter 3:9:

> The Lord is not slack concerning His promise,
> as some count slackness, but is longsuffering [or
> patient] toward us, not willing that any should per-
> ish but that all should come to repentance.

All includes us. We are called into the family of God, so the promise of receiving the gift of the Holy Spirit is ours, as well.

5

When You Are Filled

Now that we know that being filled with the Holy Spirit is for every Believer, the next question is, "What is the first thing you should do when you are filled with the Holy Spirit?" The answer to that question is very controversial, and the reason it is so controversial is that most Christians are disobedient to following what God says in His Word.

In Acts 2:1-4, we learn what happened when the first individuals were filled with the Spirit:

> When the Day of Pentecost had fully come, they were all with one accord in one place.
> And suddenly there came a sound from heaven, as of a rushing mighty wind, and it filled the whole house where they were sitting.
> Then there appeared to them divided tongues, as of fire, and one sat upon each of them.
> And they were all filled with the Holy Spirit and began to speak....

If you stopped right there, you would know what you should do when you are filled with the

Spirit. You should begin to speak. But speak what? We will get into that in a minute. Right now, I want you to notice who did the speaking:

> **And they were all filled with the Holy Spirit and began to speak....**

The people were filled, and the people spoke. The Holy Spirit did not speak. The people were the ones who did the speaking.

> **And they were all filled with the Holy Spirit and began to speak with other tongues, as the Spirit gave them utterance.**

I think we can all agree that the word *other* means "something different than what you were using before." The word *tongue* in the Greek is the word *glosse*, which means "languages." Therefore, we can read Acts 2:4 like this:

> **And they were all filled with the Holy Spirit and began to speak with languages other than their own native languages, as the Spirit gave them utterance.**

It is obvious these people spoke in languages other than their native languages. Otherwise, what they spoke would not have been other languages. Also, the inference in this verse is that when the people were filled with the Holy Spirit and spoke in other languages, those other languages must have been given to the people supernaturally by the Holy

Spirit. Just the fact that a person can speak more than one language is not supernatural. But if a person starts speaking a language other than his native tongue not only fluently, but with the right accent and intonation, and that person never studied that language, that would have to be something supernatural.

Since 1970, when I was filled with the Spirit, I have had the privilege, by the Spirit of God and the direction of Jesus, to share the Word of God in many, many places throughout the world. In all that time, the only objection I have ever encountered, relative to being filled with the Holy Spirit, has been on speaking with other tongues. This is where people's fears, confusion, and misunderstanding seem to lodge.

The main reason speaking with tongues has been a stumbling block for so many people is that they do not understand what speaking with tongues is all about. There is an aura of mystery that surrounds it, and people are usually reticent about jumping into something they do not completely understand. Many people have distorted ideas about speaking with tongues, and many of them are even fearful of it.

Also, some people may have had an encounter in church, or in some other religious context, in which someone supposedly under the influence of the Holy Spirit did something really crazy or irrational. Those people saw what was going on and said, "Man, if that is what the Holy Spirit is going to make me do, I don't want anything to do with that."

Not having "anything to do with that" is exactly what Satan wants us to do. He uses the things I have just mentioned and much more to keep Christians away from the power of the Holy Spirit. We read in the previous chapter that we need God's power for living the overcoming Christian life and for going about the King's business. Speaking with tongues is how that supernatural power is released into our lives. If we do not speak with tongues, that power is never released.

Suppose you have some money in the bank, and the bank is closed — and by "closed," I do not mean for the weekend, but "closed" as in "out of business." How much good can that money do for you? None, because you cannot write any checks or make any withdrawals to put it to use.

The same thing is true if you are filled with the Spirit and do not speak with tongues. You may have the power in the bank, but you cannot write any checks or make any withdrawals with that power, because the way you write checks and make withdrawals with the power of God is by speaking with tongues.

So the question really becomes, why tongues? Why is speaking with tongues associated with the Holy Spirit? It is associated with the Holy Spirit for two major reasons. Number one, because Jesus said so. In Mark 16:17, He says:

> "And these signs will follow those who believe: In My name they will cast out demons; they will speak with new tongues."

If someone says, "And these signs may follow," it tells us there is a possibility those signs will follow. In other words, maybe they will, and maybe they won't. But if someone says these signs will follow, it is definite.

Jesus tells us in the first part of Mark 16:17, **"And these signs will follow those who believe,"** so He is talking about what is going to follow Believers. If you are not a Believer, those signs will not follow, but if you are a Believer, they will follow. We know that to be true because Jesus says of Himself in John 14:6, **"I am the way, the truth, and the life."** He does not say He is the way and the lie.

Jesus goes on to say in the latter part of Mark 16:17, **"In My name they will cast out demons; they will speak with new tongues."** Many people have tried to say that speaking with new tongues meant that when you were a sinner, you used to curse and use all kinds of vulgar language, and when you got saved, you changed your language, so you speak with a new tongue. That is not what Jesus is saying here, however.

Just like in Acts 2:4, the word translated here as *tongues* is the Greek word *glosse*, which means "languages." Jesus is literally saying that the people who believe will speak with new languages — but they cannot and will not do that unless they are filled with the Spirit.

The church has had this thing about, "Well, some folks get filled, and some folks don't. Some folks speak with tongues, and some folks don't." If you are a Christian, you should want to please your master; therefore, you should want to be filled with the Spirit, and speak with new tongues. If you do not speak with tongues, what is your reason, because Jesus says, **"And these signs will follow those who believe"**?

Jesus also says in John 14:16-17:

> **"And I will pray the Father, and He will give you another Helper, that He may abide with you forever —**
>
> **"the Spirit of truth, whom the world cannot receive, because it neither sees Him nor knows Him; but you know Him, for He dwells with you and will be in you.**

Jesus is talking to His disciples in this statement, and every Believer is a disciple. That simply means a student, a learner, or a follower — that is all *disciple* means. It is not some special category.

The phrase *will be in you* in John 14:17 implies the Spirit of truth will be in every one of us, but He will not be in you if you do not know He exists, or if you are unwilling to receive Him. The Lord does not do anything against your will. He wants every person in the Body of Christ to be filled with the Spirit. Whether or not you are filled is up to you.

Part of the New Testament Pattern

The second confirmation that speaking with tongues is part of receiving the Holy Spirit is that it is part of the New Testament pattern. At the beginning of this chapter, we read Acts 2:4, where it says:

> **And they were all filled with the Holy Spirit and began to speak with other tongues, as the Spirit gave them utterance.**

The second account we have of people being filled with the Spirit is in the eighth chapter of Acts, starting at verse 14.

Acts 8:14-17:

> **Now when the apostles who were at Jerusalem heard that Samaria had received the word of God, they sent Peter and John to them,**
>
> **who, when they had come down, prayed for them that they might receive the Holy Spirit.**
>
> **For as yet He had fallen upon none of them. They had only been baptized in the name of the Lord Jesus.**
>
> **Then they laid hands on them, and they received the Holy Spirit.**

Notice what is conspicuous in its absence. It does not say the people spoke with other tongues when they received the Holy Spirit. But let's continue reading the story from verse 18.

Acts 8:18-21:

> And when Simon saw that through the laying on of the apostles' hands the Holy Spirit was given, he offered them money,
> saying, "Give me this power also, that anyone on whom I lay hands may receive the Holy Spirit."
> But Peter said to him, "Your money perish with you, because you thought that the gift of God could be purchased with money!
> "You have neither part nor portion in this matter, for your heart is not right in the sight of God."

After very diligent study, I found that Peter was talking in verse 21 about speaking with tongues. If you look up the Greek word translated in verse 21 as *matter*, you will learn that it is the word for *word* — not *logos*, which Bible scholars agree is a synonym for Jesus Christ, but the actual word for *word*. The verse should actually read, "You have no part nor portion in this word of utterance." That word of utterance was how Simon knew something had been imparted. He heard the people speaking with other tongues, possibly some people that he knew, and that got his attention.

Paul

In the ninth chapter of Acts, Paul (who was then called Saul) had an experience with Jesus on the Damascus road, and was sent into the city. While

Paul was in the city, God told a disciple named Ananias to go to him and pray for two things — that Paul might receive his sight (he had been blinded on the Damascus road), and that he might receive the Holy Spirit.

Acts 9:17-18:

> And Ananias went his way and entered the house; and laying his hands on him he said, "Brother Saul, the Lord Jesus, who appeared to you on the road as you came, has sent me that you may receive your sight and be filled with the Holy Spirit."
> Immediately there fell from his eyes something like scales, and he received his sight at once; and he arose and was baptized.

But what about Paul's being filled with the Holy Spirit? Ananias was instructed by the Lord to minister to Paul in that regard, and I do not know why it is not mentioned in these verses. However, we know Paul was filled with the Spirit because he wrote in 1 Corinthians 14:18, **I thank my God I speak with tongues more than you all.** Nobody else ever spoke with tongues until he or she was filled with the Spirit. We can therefore infer from what Paul wrote to the church in Corinth that he was filled with the Spirit.

This makes three separate instances in which people were filled with the Spirit and spoke with other tongues. Another incident is found in the tenth chapter of Acts, when Peter was directed by the Holy

Spirit to go to the house of a Gentile named Cornelius and minister there. In verses 44-45, we read the following:

> While Peter was still speaking these words, the Holy Spirit fell upon all those who heard the word.
>
> And those of the circumcision who believed were astonished, as many as came with Peter, because the gift of the Holy Spirit had been poured out on the Gentiles also.

Let me ask you a question. Is the Holy Spirit visible or invisible? He is invisible. How would the people who came with Peter know the Gentiles were filled if they could not see the Holy Spirit? There had to be some sort of evidence. That verse of evidence is Acts 10:46, which begins:

> For they heard....

The word *for* means the same as the word *because*.

> For [or because] they heard them speak with tongues and magnify God....

That was how the people knew that the Gentiles in Cornelius' house **"received the Holy Spirit just as we have"** (Acts 10:47). They heard the Gentiles speak with tongues. In fact, it not only convinced the people in Cornelius' house, but also the Jewish Christians Peter answered to for entering a Gentile's house in the first place (entering a Gentile's house was unlawful for a Jew). In Acts 11:15-18, we have the upshot of what happened:

> "And as I began to speak, the Holy Spirit fell upon them, as upon us at the beginning.
>
> "Then I remembered the word of the Lord, how He said, 'John indeed baptized with water, but you shall be baptized with the Holy Spirit.'
>
> "If therefore God gave them the same gift as He gave us when we believed on the Lord Jesus Christ, who was I that I could withstand God?"
>
> When they heard these things they became silent; and they glorified God, saying, "Then God has also granted to the Gentiles repentance to life."

The Jewish Christians knew all they had to do was think back to when they first believed on Jesus, and they would know how the Holy Spirit fell upon those Gentiles. The Jewish Christians spoke with tongues when the Holy Spirit fell on them, and that was exactly what happened with the Gentiles in Cornelius' house.

202/

In Ephesus

We have still another incident recorded in Acts 19, starting at verse one.

Acts 19:1-2:

> And it happened, while Apollos was at Corinth, that Paul, having passed through the upper regions, came to Ephesus. And finding some disciples
> he said to them, "Did you receive the Holy Spirit when you believed?"

Why would Paul ask these people, **"Did you receive the Holy Spirit when you believed?"** There is a difference in the atmosphere where people are gathered together who are filled with the Spirit. When you get into an environment where people are not filled with the Spirit, it is a different world altogether.

Paul came to Ephesus, and he could sense in his spirit that something was missing. It is not a feeling like an emotion, but something you can actually sense in the atmosphere. Have you ever been somewhere, and you could tell people did not like you or want you there? They did not have to put up any signs or anything. You just walked into the place, and you could feel the hostility.

That was something like what happened with Paul. He walked in there, knew something was missing, and knew exactly what it was. He knew there was a dimension of spirituality that was not there, so he asked them, **"Did you receive the Holy Spirit when you believed?"** Notice what the people told Paul in verse two:

> ... So they said to him, "We have not so much
> as heard whether there is a Holy Spirit."

Notice the word *heard*. What is significant about it is a biblical principle that is annunciated in Romans 10:17. There, Paul writes, **So then faith comes by hearing, and hearing by the word of God.**

That was why the people in Ephesus had not received the Holy Spirit. If they had not heard about the Holy Spirit, they would not have had any faith to receive Him. That is what is wrong in many churches today. The people have not really heard what the Bible says about the Holy Spirit. All they have heard is a lot of negativism — "Watch out for those tongue-talkers! Watch out for those Holy Ghost folk, because they act crazy!"

Acts 19:3-6:

> And he said to them, "Into what then were you baptized?" So they said, "Into John's baptism."
> Then Paul said, "John indeed baptized with a baptism of repentance, saying to the people that they should believe on Him who would come after him, that is, on Christ Jesus."
> When they heard this, they were baptized in the name of the Lord Jesus.
> And when Paul had laid hands on them, the Holy Spirit came upon them, and they spoke with tongues and prophesied.

In all five of these passages of scripture, we have seen illustrations of people receiving the Holy Spirit.

In three of these examples, the Bible very clearly and concisely shows that when people were filled with the Holy Spirit, they began to speak with other tongues; and in the other two passages we read, there is circumstantial evidence to indicate this happened in those situations, as well.

Someone at this point may think, "But I got filled with the Spirit, and I didn't speak with tongues." The fact you did not speak with tongues does not mean that you *could not* do it. It only means that you *did not* do it. I have known people who got married and never had any children. In a few cases, it was because of a physical challenge that precluded them from having children. But many times, it was because the couple decided they were not going to have any children. Sometimes either the husband or the wife already had children from another marriage, and those children had grown up and were on their own, so they did not feel they needed to have more children at that stage in their lives.

Also remember that in Acts 2:4, Acts 10:44-46 and Acts 19:6, it said the people were all filled with the Holy Spirit and began to speak with other tongues. Those scriptures did not say the Holy Spirit spoke, or that the Holy Spirit made the people speak. In all three instances, the people were the ones who spoke. So if you do not make an effort to speak with other tongues, you will not speak. You cannot even talk in your native language unless you put forth some effort.

"It's Not for Us"

One pivotal point where people bomb out is that they claim, "This business of being filled with the Spirit and speaking with tongues is not for everyone. It is for people who are more emotional, and for people on the lower strata of the economic totem pole." The people who make this claim consider being filled with the Spirit a purely emotional experience.

There is nothing emotional about being filled with the Holy Spirit. It is a spiritual transaction. You may respond emotionally, but being filled is not what makes you emotional. Whatever emotion you experience is *your reaction* to the experience of being filled. Because of that phenomenon, many people have been cheated out of being filled with the Holy Spirit, and the reason they were cheated is that they thought they had to be out of control emotionally to be filled with the Holy Spirit.

In all the illustrations I used to show that speaking with tongues is part of being filled with the Spirit, there is no indication that the people who were filled got emotional about it. If emotions were involved in being filled with the Spirit, certainly God would tell us what to expect, so we would know whether or not we were having the right emotion when we were filled.

Do not be afraid of being filled with the Spirit because someone acted crazy and said, "The Holy Spirit made me do it." The Holy Spirit does not make anyone do anything — ever! He has never made anyone do anything, and He will never make you do anything, because if He made someone do something, He would be violating that person's free will.

All you have to do to realize this is true is to use a little common sense. If the Holy Spirit could make you do anything, isn't it conceivable that He could make you live right? Couldn't He stop you from fornicating, committing adultery, or lying? Couldn't He make you pay your tithes? Why doesn't the Holy Spirit make people do all those things?

The Holy Spirit is not given to us to make us do anything. He is given to us to help us. Let me give you another illustration. Power steering was never designed to turn the steering wheel of your car for you. It was designed to assist you in turning the wheel. In fact, the technical term for power steering is *power assist steering*. The power steering unit will not do anything until you apply pressure to the steering wheel in a certain direction.

The Holy Spirit works the same way as power steering works in your car. He is a helper. In fact, the term *Holy Spirit* in the Greek is the word *paraclete* or *parakletos*, and it means "a helper." More specifically, it means someone who is called alongside of you to help you. The Holy Spirit will help you understand the Bible, help you pray, inspire you to go to church, and generally help you live right, but He will not do any of those things for you.

Speaking With Tongues
and Divers Kinds of Tongues

Another mistake many people make is lumping together speaking with tongues with the gift of divers kinds of tongues, one of the nine gifts of the Spirit recorded in 1 Corinthians 12. They are not the same manifestation; yet some people and churches say that speaking with tongues and the gift of tongues are one and the same, and use that as an excuse to get out of doing what the Word of God declares.

You even need to be careful about what translation of the Bible you read, because many versions of the Bible were translated by people who do not believe in speaking with tongues, or that speaking with tongues is for every Believer. For example, here is how 1 Corinthians 14:2 is translated in The Living Bible:

> **But if your gift is that of being able to "speak in tongues"....**

The way that verse is translated is incorrect, because when you are filled with the Spirit and speak with other tongues, it is not the gift of tongues. The translator is injecting a theological point of view to show that since not everyone has the same gift, not everyone has to speak with tongues. It can seem like a very clever argument to people who are not well-versed in the Word of God.

Let me show you where all the confusion has come from on this point. In 1 Corinthians 12:4-11, Paul writes:

There are diversities of gifts, but the same Spirit.

There are differences of ministries, but the same Lord.

And there are diversities of activities, but it is the same God who works all in all.

But the manifestation of the Spirit is given to each one for the profit of all:

for to one is given the word of wisdom through the Spirit, to another the word of knowledge through the same Spirit,

to another faith by the same Spirit, to another gifts of healings by the same Spirit,

to another the working of miracles, to another prophecy, to another discerning of spirits, to another different kinds of tongues, to another the interpretation of tongues.

But one and the same Spirit works all these things, distributing to each one individually as He wills.

Paul is talking here about the gift of different or divers kinds of tongues. The gift of tongues is for public assembly, and should always be accompanied by the companion gift of interpretation of tongues. The rare exception to this is when God speaks to an individual through the person doing the speaking. In other words, one person will speak with the gift of tongues, but to the person to whom the message is addressed, it will be in a language he or she will understand.

Notice also that Paul says, **To one is given the word of wisdom.** That means the word of wisdom is not given to everyone. Neither is any of the other gifts of the Spirit, including the gift of divers kinds of tongues.

Now read 1 Corinthians 12:28.

> **And God has appointed these in the church: first apostles, second prophets, third teachers, after that miracles, then gifts of healings, helps, administrations, varieties of tongues.**

What Paul is describing in this verse are the ministry gifts. There is another rendering of these gifts in the fourth chapter of Ephesians, and if you compare the lists in both of these scriptures, you will find they are the same, with one notable exception.

Notice, Paul starts out by saying **apostles.** Apostles are people, and they are a ministry gift. Then he says **prophets.** Prophets are people. Next, he says **teachers**, and teachers are people. But then Paul says **miracles, gifts of healings, helps, administrations, varieties of tongues.** Those are not people. However, they are tools that equip the people to stand in the offices of apostle, prophet, evangelist, pastor and teacher.

The gifts of the Spirit are not for everyone in the Body of Christ. They are actually for the ministry gifts God places in the Church. Nevertheless, every person in the Body of Christ who is filled with the Spirit may on occasion be used by the Spirit in any one of the manifestations of those nine gifts.

Speaking with tongues, on the other hand, is for your personal spiritual enrichment. It does not need an interpretation like the gift of tongues does, because it is simply you speaking to God. An easy way to remember the difference between speaking with tongues and the gift of tongues is that speaking with tongues is man talking to God; it goes from earth to heaven. The gift of tongues, on the other hand, comes from heaven to earth, because it is God speaking through a man to other men.

6

Benefits

How smart do you think God is? Let's say He is at least as smart as you. You want to give a person something, but you know the thing you want to give will only cause him confusion and misunderstanding. Chances are you won't give the thing to the person — especially if you know you will have to deal with him at a later date. If the person is having a hard time, you will have a hard time in dealing with him. If the person is having things go easy with him, you will have an easier time when you deal with him. Therefore, you will want to give the person something that will enhance his life and make things easier for him — not harder.

Keep that line of reasoning in mind and consider this: If speaking with tongues were not for everyone, and God were at least as smart as we are, He would know that speaking with tongues was going to be a problem for the Church. He would know that if He introduced speaking with tongues to His people, later on down the line, He would have problems, and that His family would get all messed up and be in contention with one another because of it. The best thing for God to do in that case would be not to introduce speaking with tongues into the earth-realm, or to mention anything about it. That way, there would not be any confusion.

However, God mentions in several places in His Word that we should speak with tongues when we are filled with the Spirit, so we can know what to expect when we are filled. By the same token, we can assume that there are some things about speaking with tongues from which we would gain some benefit. So what are some of those benefits?

First of all, we are told in James 3:1-2:

> My brethren, let not many of you become teachers, knowing that we shall receive a stricter judgment.
> For we all stumble in many things. If anyone does not stumble in word, he is a perfect man, able also to bridle the whole body.

In other words, if you do not cause an offense with your words, James says you are a perfect man. The word *perfect* here does not mean flawless. It means "mature or fully grown spiritually."

James goes on to say in verses three and four:

> Indeed, we put bits in horses' mouths that they may obey us, and we turn their whole body.
> Look also at ships: although they are so large and are driven by fierce winds, they are turned by a very small rudder wherever the pilot desires.

That simply means that whenever the captain turns the wheel, he is moving the rudder. Whichever way the rudder goes, that is the way the ship goes. The rudder is tiny compared to the overall size of the ship, yet that little rudder can control that ship and determine its direction.

Likewise, a horse is much larger than the person who rides it, yet with a bridle and bit in the horse's mouth, the person can pull on the reins to the right or to the left, and the horse will go in the direction the rider pulls. A horse is very easy to control by moving its head, so if you turn its head, it will go in the direction its head is turned.

Keep all this in mind, and read verses five through eight:

> **Even so the tongue is a little member and boasts great things. See how great a forest a little fire kindles!**
> **And the tongue is a fire, a world of iniquity. The tongue is so set among our members that it defiles the whole body, and sets on fire the course of nature; and it is set on fire by hell.**
> **For every kind of beast and bird, of reptile and creature of the sea, is tamed and has been tamed by mankind.**
> **But no man can tame the tongue. It is an unruly evil, full of deadly poison.**

Can you see the spiritual implication here? Your tongue is very small compared to the rest of your body, but it can ruin your life. Your tongue has probably gotten you into more trouble than anything else. So isn't it interesting that the first thing the Holy Spirit takes over in your life when you receive Him into your spirit is the one thing you cannot control?

One of the ways through which we as Christians have done the most damage to one another is with our mouths. I have been walking by the Word of God for many, many years now, and for all that time, I have not had one person hit me with his or her fist in the mouth. I have not even been punched in the stomach. No one has laid a physical hand on me. But I have been bruised countless times by Christians saying things with their mouths that they did not even know were true or false. Just because some other ignorant person said it, they picked it up and started saying it.

The only reason why what people have said about me has not bothered me is that I do not let it bother me. If I did let it bother me, it would hurt me very badly. Sometimes, I have had people say things about me when I have tried to help them. I remember doing my best, one time even laying awake at night trying to figure out how to help a particular person, and then the person ended up talking about me like a dog — talked about me like I had a tail, then talked about me concerning some things the person had no knowledge about.

I have also had situations where ministers who did not even know me would talk negatively about me on radio or television, or write about me in a book. It would not have been so bad if they knew me or had been in my company for any length of time.

But most of these ministers had never even met me. They would take something out of context from a cassette tape or from one of my books, and try to make something out of it.

The worst thing about what these ministers did is that they never thought that what they printed or were saying may have destroyed the confidence of someone who has believed some of the things I have taught, and who may have had his or her life changed for the better.

I may personally disagree with many ministers, and with a lot of teaching that I hear, but I do not get on the person. I leave it alone, because maybe that teaching is helping someone. Not everything is for Fred, and I do not have to receive everything. It is just like choosing an automobile. There are certain kinds and models of cars I would not drive. There are some cars I do not like the look of, even though they may be the best cars in the world from an engineering standpoint. The car manufacturer did not make that car for Fred. They made it for all the other people who are buying the car and keeping the company in business. So why should I get a big sign or write a book and say you should not make that kind of car?

We have said things to our children that have crushed them. It may not matter if anyone else says anything negative about you, but for your mother or father to say it to you is another matter. You could have taken getting shot in the arm with a gun better than for your mother to say, "You ain't no good.

You're just like your old daddy. He was a drunk, his daddy was a drunk, and you'll probably be a drunk just like him." Some people have carried around things like that for much of their lives.

Words can destroy people. That is one of the reasons the Lord wants you to be filled with the Spirit with the evidence of speaking with other tongues. When you are filled, you can learn over a period of time how to yield your tongue to the Holy Spirit. That is something you have to do by faith. You do not know what you are going to say, so you have to yield your tongue strictly as an act of faith. That will help you, in turn, to yield your tongue to the Word of God.

Speaking Directly to God

The second benefit we can receive from speaking with tongues is found in 1 Corinthians 14:2:

> **For he who speaks in a tongue does not speak to men but to God, for no one understands him; however, in the spirit he speaks mysteries.**

A better translation for the word *mysteries* in the Greek would be *divine secrets*. Now notice, in the latter part of this verse:

> **... for no one understands him; however, in the spirit....**

Many people who have accused us "tongue talkers" of being fanatical and emotional like to think of themselves as being very spiritual. That is why they think they can afford to shoot us down. But the Word of God says, **... for no one understands him; however, in the spirit he speaks** [divine secrets]. It is the person speaking with tongues who is in the Spirit, not the critic.

In the fourth chapter of John, Jesus had an encounter with a Samaritan woman at Jacob's well, just outside the city of Sychar. The bottom line was that they talked about things that had to do with the Almighty, and the lady asked Jesus a question. She said, in essence, "You Jews say that in Jerusalem is the place to worship, but our forefathers told us that the place to actually worship God is here in the mountains of Samaria. What do you say about it?" Jesus answered her question in John 4:23-24 by saying this:

> **"But the hour is coming, and now is, when the true worshipers will worship the Father in spirit and truth; for the Father is seeking such to worship Him.**
>
> **"God is Spirit, and those who worship Him must worship in spirit and truth."**

Notice the words, **"... worship in spirit and truth."** That echoes what Paul said in 1 Corinthians: **... however, in the spirit he speaks mysteries.** Another scripture that ties into this idea is Hebrews 12:9, where Paul says:

> Furthermore, we have had human fathers who corrected us, and we paid them respect. Shall we not much more readily be in subjection to the Father of spirits and live?

Isn't it interesting that Paul does not say "the Father of flesh and blood," but **the Father of spirits.** The word *spirits* is in small case, which means Paul is talking about the spirit of man. God is not the Father of your flesh and blood. God is the Father of you, and you are a spirit.

You may have heard people say, "Well, I'm just flesh and blood. What do you expect?" But that statement is not really true. You are a spirit, and you live inside of a flesh-and-blood body. You are not flesh and blood. In fact, there is an easy way to prove this. All you have to do is go to the cemetery, unearth some caskets, and see how many live people you run into.

If you were flesh and blood, then those bodies in the cemetery should all be alive. You are a spirit. That is the part of you that is real. However, God is your Father only when you are His child, and you are not His child unless you are adopted into His family. You cannot be adopted into His family without going through adoption procedures. Jesus Christ is the head of the adoption agency, and you have to go through Him to be adopted into the family of God. When you do that, then God becomes your Father, the Father of your spirit.

Now, your Father has devised a method by which your spirit can talk to Him as a spirit without your flesh and blood getting in the way. This is very desirable, because sometimes our flesh gets in the way. Sometimes our heads get in the way. Our minds, the soul-part of us, mess us up in many areas. So how can our spirits talk with God without our minds messing up the connection? Read 1 Corinthians 14:2 once more:

> **For he who speaks in a tongue does not speak to men but to God, for no one understands him; however, in the spirit he speaks mysteries.**

Speaking with tongues is how our spirits can talk with God. People say things like, "Well, I want to get into the spirit." Speaking with tongues is how you do that.

Edifying Yourself

While we are in 1 Corinthians 14, I want us to read the fourth verse:

> **He who speaks in a tongue edifies himself....**

The word *edify* is one we do not use much in modern English. The best word in English that gives the essence of what Paul is saying here is *charge*, as in charging a battery.

You may have had an experience when you went to start up your car and the battery was dead. You did not take the battery to the cemetery and bury it. You probably had someone attach some jumper cables from your car to his to start your car; then you drove your car to a place where they could put the battery on a charger. It took some time to charge up the electrical energy in the battery, but as long as you kept your battery charged up, it would always start your car.

What God has devised is a method by which your spiritual batteries can stay charged up. That way, your batteries will stay strong, and you will always be able to "turn over" the engine of your life.

I am so grateful that Paul says I can edify myself, because people in general are flaky. You cannot count on them. They might be up today and down tomorrow. They might be in today and out tomorrow, or here today and gone tomorrow. I am not saying that I do not love them. I just do not like to depend on them for my spiritual enrichment and edification. So I am just thrilled to life that my heavenly Father has provided a way through which I can stay spiritually strong without having to depend on other people.

Too many people do not take the time to "charge up" their spiritual batteries. They let their batteries run down and get into situations where they do not have any power to spare. That is why many people are living "dead engine" lives — because they are not charged up. You should be charged up, and you can be that way if you learn how to speak with other tongues.

Another verse that talks about charging ourselves up is Jude 20:

**But you, beloved, building yourselves up on
your most holy faith, praying in the Holy Spirit.**

Build up in this verse means the same as to
"charge up." You pray in the Holy Spirit by praying
with other tongues. However, notice what Jude does
not say. He does not say that praying in the Holy
Spirit will *give you* faith. He says it will *build you up*
on your most holy faith. You already have the faith
if you are born-again, but praying in the Holy Spirit
will build you up on that faith.

Jude also does not say someone else will build
you up. That is where many Christians make a
mistake. They are always looking for someone else
to build them up. Many people go to church to be
built up. They come to be inspired. They come to be
pumped up, to get a spiritual shot of adrenaline.

I do not come to church for that purpose. I come
to church charged up. I go to church inspired. I live
inspired. I have had plenty of opportunities to be
down — they come all the time — but I just let them
pass on by.

Letting Your Spirit Pray

In the first part of 1 Corinthians 14:14, Paul tells us:

For if I pray in a tongue, my spirit prays....

We use the term *speaking with tongues*, but you
just do not go around and start talking with tongues

when you see someone. Actually, speaking with tongues is prayer. It is the voice of your spirit talking to your Father.

If you flip this verse around, you could say that if you do not pray in a tongue, your spirit does not pray. Think of the multitude of Christians who go through their whole lives without letting their spirits pray. It does not mean they do not love the Lord, or that they will not go to heaven when they die. What it means is that they are getting cheated out of a lot of things God wants them to have that would enrich their lives.

Paul continues in 1 Corinthians 14:14 by saying:

For if I pray in a tongue, my spirit prays, but my understanding is unfruitful.

Your understanding is your mind, which is located in the soul part of your three-fold nature. Contained in the soul part of your nature are your mind, your will, your desires and your emotions. That is what makes up your personality.

Paul adds in 1 Corinthians 14:15:

What is the conclusion then? I will pray with the spirit, and I will also pray with the under-standing. I will sing with the spirit, and I will also sing with the understanding.

We can pray with the spirit, and we can pray with the understanding. And there is a time when you want to pray with the understanding. If we are getting ready to eat some food, and I am going to pray over it, I want you to be in agreement with me. But if I pray with other tongues, you will not know what I said, so you will not be able to agree with me. This is a case where I would have to pray with my understanding. If I want to edify myself, then I pray with the spirit.

You might ask yourself, "Why does the Lord have it so I don't understand what I am saying when I speak with tongues?" Let me ask you this: Have you ever been praying in English, and while you were praying, some thought you were not intentionally thinking came to your mind? You are telling God how much you love Him, you are asking Him certain things, and here comes this thought from somewhere out of left field. You have to deal with that thought so you can get back on track and finish praying.

When you pray with other tongues, there is no way that could ever happen. You do not know what you are saying; therefore, you cannot monitor the language yourself. You cannot mess it up, and neither can Satan — even though Satan is the one who brings those thoughts your way.

Not Walking in the Flesh

You cannot pray with other tongues if you have not been filled with the Spirit. As I mentioned earlier in this book, there are two transactions the Bible talks about: one is being born of the Spirit, and the other is being filled with the Spirit. Many people lump those transactions together, but you really cannot do that without cheating yourself. A passage of scripture that will help illustrate this is Romans 8:9. There, Paul writes:

> **But you are not in the flesh but in the Spirit, if indeed the Spirit of God dwells in you. Now if anyone does not have the Spirit of Christ, he is not His.**

You can understand from reading this verse why some people say, "I'm filled with the Holy Spirit, even though I don't speak with other tongues. I've got to be filled with the Holy Spirit, because the Word says if I don't have the Spirit of God in me, I am not His, and I know I've been born again." Romans 8:9 is the verse people have used to prove this point, but the people who made the point missed what Paul was really saying here.

To get the full impact of what Paul is saying, let's go back to Romans 8:1. Paul begins there by writing:

> **There is therefore now no condemnation** [or judgment] **to those who are in Christ Jesus....**

If Paul had put a period there, what he states in Romans 8:1 would undoubtedly refer to every Christian. But there is no period there, and there should not be one. Instead, Paul writes in verses one through five:

> There is therefore now no condemnation to those who are in Christ Jesus, who do not walk according to the flesh, but according to the Spirit.
>
> For the law of the Spirit of life in Christ Jesus has made me free from the law of sin and death.
>
> For what the law could not do in that it was weak through the flesh, God did by sending His own Son in the likeness of sinful flesh, on account of sin: He condemned sin in the flesh,
>
> that the righteous requirement of the law might be fulfilled in us who do not walk according to the flesh but according to the Spirit.
>
> For those who live according to the flesh set their minds on the things of the flesh, but those who live according to the Spirit....

Paul is talking here about the difference between Christians who walk by the flesh, and Christians who walk by the spirit. There are many Christians who are called carnal Christians (carnal comes from the word *carne*, which means "meat" or "flesh"), and they live their whole lives in the flesh. It does not mean they are not saved, or that God does not love them. It simply means they cannot live at God's best — and God wants us to live at His best.

Paul goes on in Romans 8:5-6 by saying this:

> For those who live according to the flesh set their minds on the things of the flesh, but those who live according to the Spirit, the things of the Spirit.
>
> For to be carnally minded is death, but to be spiritually minded is life and peace.

Every minute you live, you are getting closer to the graveyard than you were when you started this physical life. When you walk in the flesh as a Christian, it escalates the rate of death that is working in your life, because your mind is dead, and it is going to speak death to you. Operating in the Spirit will retard that rate of death, and extend your life. That is what Paul means by the statement, **For to be carnally minded is death.**

It is very easy to tell which Christians are carnally minded, and which Christians are spiritually minded. People who come to church late all the time are carnally minded. If they were spiritually minded Christians empowered by the Holy Spirit, they would be on time. To bicker, gripe, grumble and complain is carnal, because bickering, griping, grumbling and complaining does not come out of your spirit. Always finding fault with the church, instead of praying for the church and supporting it, is carnal; and anyone who gossips about something, especially about something bad, is acting in a carnal manner. Gossiping is something your flesh does, not your spirit.

Paul adds in Romans 8:7-9:

> Because the carnal mind is enmity against God; for it is not subject to the law of God, nor indeed can be.
> So then, those who are in the flesh cannot please God.
> But you are not in the flesh but in the Spirit, if indeed the Spirit of God dwells in you....

The phrase **if indeed the Spirit of God dwells in you** indicates that the Holy Spirit might not be dwelling in you. If His dwelling in you were automatic, Paul would not have to say *if.*

When Paul says, in the latter part of verse nine, **Now if anyone does not have the Spirit of Christ, he is not His,** he is talking about salvation. But when he says, **... if indeed the Spirit of God dwells in you,** he is talking about being filled with the Spirit. The Holy Spirit will not dwell in you unless you invite Him to come in and take up residence in your spirit. And when you invite Him to come in and live within you, you will be able to speak with other tongues. If you do not speak with other tongues, you have not finished the transaction.

Helping in Our Weaknesses

Let me show you another benefit of being filled with the Spirit, and why you need to release the power of the Spirit into your life through speaking with tongues. In Romans 8:26, Paul starts out by saying this:

> **Likewise the Spirit also helps in our weaknesses. For we do not know what we should pray for as we ought....**

Many people misquote this verse, and say, "You know, the Bible says we don't know how to pray, so we need to do thus-and-so." That is not what Paul is saying. If the bill collector sends me a notice saying he is going to foreclose on my house unless I give him $3,000, I ought to pray for $3,000. If I am starving and do not have any money to buy food, I ought to pray for some food, or for some money with which to buy it. If I do not have a job, I ought to pray for a job that will pay me enough money to take care of me and my family.

What Paul is saying is that we do not always know *what to pray for* as we ought. This applies only to intercessory prayer, where your total prayer is on the behalf of and for the benefit of someone else.

Most of the Christian prayer life is "My name is Jimmy, I'll take all you'll give me." It is basically me, myself and I. We should learn to pray for other people, to intercede on their behalf — and intercession means taking some time. It does not mean saying "Well, bless him, Lord" and leaving. That is what most people do — "Oh, go to the prisons and all the hospitals, Lord, and bless the people. Oh, hallelujah." That is not intercession. That is a joke.

The reason the Holy Spirit helps and leads you in intercession is that, in many cases, you do not know what you are praying for or praying about. There is a general kind of intercession you can make, such as praying for leaders and other people in authority. But there is also a deeper kind of intercession that goes beyond your actual knowledge of the facts. All you know is that somehow, on the inside of you, you know that you have to pray. That is when the Holy

Spirit helps you to pray as you ought. How does the Holy Spirit help you? Paul tells us in the latter part of Romans 8:26:

> ... but the Spirit Himself makes intercession for us with groanings which cannot be uttered.

If the Holy Spirit makes intercession for us with groanings which cannot be uttered, how could they be groanings? Groaning by definition is uttering something. The essence of what Paul writes here, in the original Greek, is that the groanings made by the Holy Spirit cannot be uttered in articulate speech. In other words, they cannot be uttered in our native languages. That is because our native vocabulary runs out, and there is nothing else we can say. But when we pray with other tongues, we can say everything that needs to be said.

Romans 8:26-27:

> Likewise the Spirit also helps in our weaknesses. For we do not know what we should pray for as we ought, but the Spirit Himself makes intercession for us with groanings which cannot be uttered.
> Now He who searches the hearts knows what the mind of the Spirit is, because He makes intercession for the saints according to the will of God.

Things have to be prayed for in the earth-realm. You may wonder why the world is as messed up as it is. A lot of it is because of Christians abdicating their responsibility to pray. In many cases, it is really more a case of ignorance, because most churches do not tell people how to pray — and that is just a fact.

God cannot do anything in the earth-realm without our permission. He does not own the earth by right of occupancy. He legally owns the earth because of what Jesus did at Calvary, and because of Jesus' resurrection from the dead. But God is not yet able to occupy the earth because there was a lease placed on it by Adam in the Garden of Eden. The ownership of the earth has changed, but the lease is still in force, and God cannot evict the lease-holder until the lease has run its course.

Many people have a problem with that concept. We have always had the idea in Christianity that God could do anything He wants to do, and in a sense, He can. In terms of power, God can do anything. In fact, if God wanted to, He could save people without their believing in Jesus. There is nothing in the Bible that says He cannot do that. It is just the way He has designed the system.

However, God has limited Himself by His Word. If His Word is forever settled in heaven — and He has said that it is — He cannot violate it. God has set things to work in an orderly fashion, and He of all people has to abide by the Word that He gave, or else He reduces Himself to the level of man. Most of the time, our word is no good. We say one thing Monday and do something else on Tuesday. But the Bible says that God is the same yesterday, today, and forever.

A scripture that shows who has been holding "the lease" on the earth all this time is Luke 4:1, 2, 5, 6 and 7:

> Then Jesus, being filled with the Holy Spirit, returned from the Jordan and was led by the Spirit into the wilderness,
> being tempted for forty days by the devil....
> Then the devil, taking Him up on a high mountain, showed Him all the kingdoms of the world in a moment of time.
> And the devil said to Him, "All this authority I will give You, and their glory; for this has been delivered to me, and I give it to whomever I wish.
> "Therefore, if You will worship before me, all will be Yours."

The devil did not say he crept up behind someone with a lead pipe one night, fractured the person's head, and stole the authority. He did not say someone sent him the authority by mail-order catalog. He said, **"All this authority ... has been delivered to me, and I give it to whomever I wish."** That is a powerful statement.

Where and when was that authority delivered to the devil? In the Garden of Eden, when Adam ate the forbidden fruit. That is part of the reason Jesus had to come to the earth-realm. Part of the reason was to redeem mankind, but in redeeming man, He was also to redeem the earth.

Here is something else that will prove my point. Jesus says in John 3:16, **"For God so loved the world that He gave His only begotten Son, that whoever** believes in Him should not perish but have everlasting life." We can say from that statement that people becoming saved is the will of God. After all, He is the one who started salvation. It is His project. However, we have this statement in Matthew 9:37-38:

> Then He [Jesus] said to His disciples, "The harvest truly is plentiful, but the laborers are few. "Therefore pray the Lord of the harvest to send out laborers into His harvest."

Why would we have to pray that God Almighty would send laborers into a harvest He created? Why would we have to pray about salvation when the Bible says, **"For God so loved the world..."**? It is because God cannot come into this earth-realm unless He has permission.

We have a legal right to be here, because mankind was fashioned from the dust of the earth, and we are the children of God. Therefore, we can invite our Father into the earth-realm through intercessory prayer, by praying in the spirit, so God can move on the hearts of people, and send out laborers into His harvest.

7

Questions and Answers

When you teach on an area as neglected and misunderstood as the Holy Spirit, there are always questions that arise in the minds of the people. At many churches, unfortunately, you do not get many answers to your questions. In fact, you get a lot of reasons to have questions, and not much explanation in reference to the things of God. So what I would like to do now is deal with some questions that have come up over the years about the Holy Spirit.

1. *How do I know that I'm not making these words up when I speak with tongues?*

That is a valid question. Let me pose a few questions in response. Why don't you have some faith in your faith? Why don't you have some faith in your own integrity? Was it your purpose to make up those words? Probably not. Did you plan to make up those words? Again, probably not. So why do you want to let the devil cheat you out of something by telling you that you made up words when that was not your intent?

"But I know a lot of people who just made a mockery out of it. They made those words up."

So what? I know a lot of people who have gotten a divorce, but I am not going to get one. The fact that some man or woman gets a divorce does not invalidate the institution of marriage. It does not make marriage illegal or unobtainable. So even if someone you came in contact with made up the words when he or she supposedly spoke with tongues, trust yourself. Have faith in your own integrity.

Besides that, all you have to do is stop and listen to yourself. When you are filled with the Spirit, you are like a baby spiritually, and at first your heavenly language may sound like baby talk. When I was first filled with the Spirit, all I could make was one sound. I didn't know why my lips would not or did not form any words, and I was embarrassed. To me, I sounded like a fool. But I knew my heart, and I knew I was not playing games with God.

I was frustrated that what came out of my mouth did not sound like a language to me, but I was convinced that speaking with tongues was of the Lord, and so I finally got before the Lord about it. I told Him, "What I am doing sounds dumb to me. It sounds stupid, and I would be embarrassed for anyone else to hear me doing this. I don't sound like I have one iota of intelligence. But Father, You

are the one who filled me with the Holy Spirit. It's the Holy Spirit who gives me the utterance; I simply add the sound and lend my tongue and vocal cords to You. If this is speaking with tongues, I don't like the way it sounds. It doesn't sound too cool to me, but if You like it and you can stand it, I'm going to give it back to You until You give me something better."

At the suggestion of my wife's Aunt Tena, I went with her to the final meeting of a revival they were having at her church. The man leading the service was Dr. Robert Frost, author of the book *Aglow With the Spirit.* At the conclusion of the service, Dr. Frost inquired if there were any who needed ministering to, and something on the inside of me said, "Have them pray for you." That was the Holy Spirit.

Immediately, Satan spoke up, and these thoughts crossed my mind: "I can't have anyone pray for me. I would be repudiating everything that happened to me when I first received the Holy Spirit. I'm a minister of the Gospel. I should be praying for others instead of them praying for me."

No one responded to the offer of ministry, so Dr. Frost started to turn the service over to the minister of the church. He asked once more if anyone needed to be ministered to. Again, the voice on the inside said, "Have them pray for you." And again, Satan spoke up to talk me out of it. By now we had joined hands and formed a circle to dismiss.

The minister was praying the closing prayer, and I knew this was it — it was now or never. As the amen was spoken and we had just loosed our hands,

I fell to my knees in the center of the circle, and poured out my heart in tears. The group moved in; I felt many hands on my head and heard many voices raised in prayer on my behalf. I opened my mouth and torrents of unknown words poured out of my mouth. In faith I had spoken and the Holy Spirit had given me the utterance.

Again, have faith in your own integrity. You will know you are not making it up when you speak with tongues. It is the Spirit of God, and your language will change. Mine changed and developed over the years. So do not be afraid. Give any misgivings you may have about it to the Lord.

2. Can I be edified by thinking of the spiritual words, and not have to say them?

Again, let me answer by asking a question. What is the primary purpose or focus for speaking with tongues? Prayer. Prayer is prayer, whether you pray with your spirit or with your understanding (in your native language).

In Luke 11:2, Jesus tells the disciples this:

So He said to them, "When you pray, say:..."

When you pray, you have to say something. That is why Jesus says in Mark 11:23, **"For assuredly, I say to you, whoever says to this mountain, 'Be removed and be cast into the sea,' and does not doubt in his heart, but believes that those things he**

says will be done, he will have whatever he says." It is the saying that puts your faith and God to work on the situation.

It is also one reason Paul writes in 1 Corinthians 14:4, **He who speaks in a tongue edifies himself....** He says, "He who speaks," not "he who thinks." It is obvious by what is not said that just thinking your heavenly language does not work. If you are edified by speaking, then you must not be edified if you do not speak.

This idea of saying when you pray is true for all kinds of prayer. When I was first saved, I wanted everything that God had for me, so I went to every meeting at the church my wife and I attended. It just so happened that they had a prayer meeting in the church Wednesday nights, so my wife and I went. They would sing a few songs, the deacon would take prayer requests, and I can remember people standing and saying, "Brother So-and-So, I have a silent request."

We just read in Luke 11:2, out of the mouth of Jesus, that when you pray, you should say something aloud. That means if you do not say anything, you are not praying, and you will not get any results.

"Well, Brother Price, I disagree with that. I had it in my heart, and even though I didn't say it, God knows I had it in my heart."

God also knows you are the biggest liar on this side of town, because Jesus says in Matthew 12:34, **"For out of the abundance of the heart the mouth** speaks." If the mouth is not speaking, there must not be anything in your heart. If something were there, it would come out of your mouth.

There is no such thing as an unspoken request. If you think an unspoken request works with God, the next time you need gasoline, drive up to the full service island at your local gas station. When the attendant comes to your car, roll down your window and tell him, "I have an unspoken request," and see how much gas you get in your car.

We can understand that illustration, but we still have this idea that God is some kind of cosmic bell-hop who does not have anything else to do but run around taking orders from us. That is not the case.

If you want God to hear and answer your prayer, you have to pray according to the Book, according to the rules laid out by Jesus in the Word. Jesus says, **"When you pray, say."** Paul says, **He who speaks in a tongue edifies himself....** So he who only thinks does nothing for himself. If you do not speak, you will not be edified.

3. *When will I be able to speak like you do?*

Probably never, because your motivation is out of line. What does it matter whether or not you ever speak like I do? Why would you want to speak like me? Be yourself. I thought you were talking to the Lord, so what difference does it make what you sound like?

I have been some places and heard people talk in a language other than English, and wondered, "My goodness, could that be a language?" And it must have been. Either that or they were sure putting on a good show, because the people who were talking acted like they understood one another. To me, it did not sound like anything, so you cannot go by how something sounds.

We just read in 1 Corinthians 14:4:

> **He who speaks in a tongue edifies himself....**

Paul adds in the 14th verse of the same chapter:

> **For if I pray in a tongue, my spirit prays....**

Speaking with tongues can be all kinds of different languages. In 1 Corinthians 13, Paul gives a slight amount of revelation about it when he says in verse one:

> **Though I speak with the tongues of men and of angels....**

We might be speaking in the tongue of another man, or we might be speaking in the tongues of angels. But what difference does it make which tongue you are speaking in, as long as you get your message through, and as long as you receive edification?

One thing I am certain about is that the more you speak in your heavenly language, the more fluent you will become. Besides that, you will become more accustomed to hearing it, so it will become more familiar to you. It will sound more coherent the more you use it, so do not be concerned about how it sounds now. Just speak. By faith, open your mouth and speak. The Holy Spirit will give you the language — just speak it out.

Do not let yourself be deceived. Before I started Crenshaw Christian Center, there was a lady who came to the church I was pastoring who had gotten filled with the Holy Spirit. She did not believe that she had been filled, so I asked her what made her think that. She said, "Well, pastor, I just don't think I'm filled because it just doesn't sound like this is the real thing." So I said, "Go ahead and pray in the Spirit, and let me listen to you."

This woman had the most beautiful manifestation of speaking with tongues. My speaking with tongues sounded like a bunch of babies in a nursery. She spoke just like people normally speak in their native language. She had the most beautiful enunciation, and her words were fabulous. But because she did not get knocked off of her chair emotionally when she prayed, she did not think she was really speaking with tongues.

I told this woman, "Lady, trust me. You are filled with the Spirit." But as far as I know, to this day, that lady has never accepted that. She said, "I don't believe it," because she did not have the emotions going with it. So don't be concerned about what your language sounds like. Just give it to your

Father, and when He gets tired of it, He will give you another dialect. He must be pleased to hear the language you are using, because He gave it to you.

4. *Can the devil give me words to say in the spirit? How do I know what I am saying is not from the devil?*

Let's look at something Jesus said in Luke 11:9-13:

> "So I say to you, ask, and it will be given to you; seek, and you will find; knock, and it will be opened to you.
> "For everyone who asks receives, and he who seeks finds, and to him who knocks it will be opened.
> "If a son asks for bread from any father among you, will he give him a stone? Or if he asks for a fish, will he give him a serpent instead of a fish?
> "Or if he asks for an egg, will he offer him a scorpion?
> "If you then, being evil, know how to give good gifts to your children, how much more will your heavenly Father give the Holy Spirit to those who ask Him!"

If you have asked God in faith, trust that the devil cannot tamper with your prayer language. He cannot get in — not on this, he can't. He is locked out. When you speak with tongues, that is not the devil. However, the devil wants you to think that your special language is coming from him. That is why he will pop that thought into your mind. That way, he will stop you from praying.

Satan cannot make you do anything. The only thing he can do is suggest. That is all the devil can do, and that is all the Father will do. Why do you think God gave you His Word? The Book is there simply to influence your will. It is your will that makes the difference.

God wants you to be strong. That is why He tells us through Paul to pray with other tongues. He says it so you will build yourself up, and become strong in the Spirit and in the power of Almighty God. That way, the devil will not be able to do a thing against you.

Likewise, Satan will try to come with all kinds of things to confuse and influence you. If he can get you to doubt that you are filled with the Holy Spirit, or that what you are speaking is not inspired by the Holy Spirit, he will stop you from edifying yourself. And when you stop edifying yourself, you will be a pushover for his temptations, trials, and tests. Do not fall for it.

5. *How do I know that God really wants me to speak with tongues?*

There are many scriptures I could use to deal with that, but I want to use something a little different, that will make it abundantly clear to you as an individual that God wants you to speak with tongues. The Book of Jude starts out with this statement:

> Jude, a bondservant of Jesus Christ, and brother of James,
> To those who are called, sanctified by God the Father, and preserved in Jesus Christ.

To whom is Jude writing this letter? To those who are sanctified by God, and preserved in Jesus Christ. That is not talking about ministers. Every person in the world is called by God to sonship with Him through Jesus Christ. That is the calling Jude is talking about here.

In the fourth chapter of Ephesians, Paul starts out with a very interesting statement that has to do with what we just read in Jude. He says in the first three verses:

> I, therefore, the prisoner of the Lord, beseech you to walk worthy of the calling with which you were called,
> with all lowliness and gentleness, with longsuffering, bearing with one another in love,
> endeavoring to keep the unity of the Spirit in the bond of peace.

Now let's go over to Ephesians 1:1:

> Paul, an apostle of Jesus Christ by the will of God,
> To the saints who are in Ephesus, and faithful in Christ Jesus.

That refers to every person at every age, at every time, on every continent who is in Christ — not just to the people who were physically in Ephesus when Paul wrote the letter. With that in mind, read Ephesians 4:1 again:

> **I, therefore, the prisoner of the Lord, beseech you....**

You who? You who are Christ's. Not just the ones who are physically in Ephesus, but everyone in Christ.

> **I, therefore, the prisoner of the Lord, beseech you to walk worthy of the calling with which you were called....**

He is talking about the fact that every person in Christ is called. That is how they got in Christ — by being called into Him by God through the Gospel. Not called to preach the Gospel as an apostle, prophet, evangelist, pastor, or teacher. Certainly, everyone is called to tell the Good News, but not everyone is called to stand in the office of ministry. But we are called, and that is how we got into the Body of Christ — by someone calling us through the preaching of the Gospel.

Now go back to Jude 1:1.

> **Jude, a bondservant of Jesus Christ, and brother of James,**
> To those who are called, sanctified....

The word *sanctified* is a great big theological term. All it means is "set apart." I can remember when I was younger the people I knew did not have a lot of money, and they did not have 25 changes of bed linens and things like that. My mother and grandmother and people like that had special linen — sheets, pillow cases and blankets they did not use every day. They saved those things for out-of-town guests, special occasions, or when someone got sick, so the doctor would not see any dirty linens when he came to the house on a housecall.

That is what *sanctification* literally means. It means "set apart to a holy service." Being a child of God is a "special occasion," and you do not have to do anything to sanctify yourself.

There are some churches and some people whom I remember being called "sanctified folk." When someone used that term, the person used it sarcastically, because these people usually dressed a certain way or fixed their hair a certain way that was quite a bit different from the average. But as I just mentioned, only God can set you apart. Sanctification is God's responsibility. Holiness is our responsibility. Sanctification is the place you have in God through Christ. Holiness is the quality of life you live in Christ.

Jude, a bondservant of Jesus Christ, and brother of James,
To those who are called, sanctified by God the Father, and preserved in Jesus Christ.

We found out in Ephesians that we are called to sonship with God. Everyone is called to be a son of God, so this is talking to those people in the Body of Christ.

Now while we are in Jude, let's read the 20th verse.

> But you....

Who does you refer to? To those who are sanctified by God.

> **But you, beloved, building yourselves up on your most holy faith, praying in the Holy Spirit.**

Praying in the Holy Spirit means praying with other tongues, because the way you pray in the Holy Spirit is to pray with other tongues. You, as I just pointed out, refers to everyone in the Body of Christ. Jude does not say, "But a few of you." He says, **But you**. "You" means all those of us who are sanctified.

6. *Why don't I feel anything when I am speaking with tongues?*

I have had that question asked many times. As I mentioned earlier, I have had some people who really thought they were not filled because they did not feel anything. They had the idea that something of this magnitude, being filled with the Spirit, just had to be associated with great emotional upheavals within themselves. I have also been in situations before I was filled with the Spirit, where people would be jumping all over the church acting crazy while speaking with tongues. That was one of the things that initially frightened me away from tongues. I thought, "If I have to do that in front of the church, forget it."

You have to realize one very important fact: The Holy Spirit will never make you do anything outside of your character. In fact, He will never make you do anything, period.

Here is the best illustration I can think of to prove this point. Chances are, at some point in your life, you have reached for something and not realized what you were reaching for was flame-hot. You grabbed ahold of it and immediately reacted by letting go. The heat did not make you do that. That was simply your reaction to the situation.

My point is this: We are all different, and because of who you are, you may react differently when you are filled with the Spirit than someone else. However, it is not the Holy Spirit making you or anyone else react in a particular way. What you do is *your* reaction to His infilling.

If you are ordinarily a calm person, you may be calm when you are speaking with tongues. If you are ordinarily a highly emotional person, you may be highly emotional when you speak with tongues. That is *you* making you react that way. It is your nature, and there is nothing right or wrong about it.

We have to look to the Word of God, not to someone's reaction. When you speak with tongues, it is a spiritual exercise. It is not soulish, nor physical, so you are not necessarily supposed to feel anything emotionally. That is because what you are doing is not based in the area of your emotions. You could have no emotion whatsoever when you speak with tongues, and your speaking would be spiritually valid.

Your not feeling anything from an emotional point of view does not invalidate the fact that you are actually speaking with tongues, or that the Holy Spirit is actually moving in you. Therefore, do not be concerned if you do not feel anything. Your speaking with tongues is just as real and valid as if you shake, jump, twist, or do anything else while you are speaking. And if you go through any of those physical actions or experience something emotionally when you speak with tongues, chalk it up as a fringe benefit.

7. *What do you do when someone tells you, "I don't think that I am speaking"?*

I have dealt many times with people who have said that. You can ask the person to speak with tongues, and the person speaks with no problem whatsoever. You then ask the individual what he or she just did, and the person will say, "I don't know." As I mentioned when answering the previous question, the person probably did not feel a great emotional charge when he or she spoke with tongues. Therefore, he is left with the impression that he did not do anything of consequence.

How emotionally charged up do you feel when you talk in your native language? You probably do not feel charged up at all, because generally, your speaking in your native language is not emotional. You are merely communicating. Likewise, when you speak with tongues, you are communicating with your heavenly Father. You are imparting information from your spirit to God. So believe, when you speak, that you are speaking.

I personally believe that one of the reasons the Father gave us the gift of the Holy Spirit with the evidence of speaking with tongues is that speaking with tongues is one of the greatest developers of faith that there is. That is because you have to speak by faith. You do not know what you are going to say when you open your mouth, and if you have any doubt about speaking with tongues, you will not be able to speak. You have to do it by faith.

I also believe one of the reasons I have been able to develop my faith to the extent that I have is that I have spent so much time speaking with tongues, praying in the Spirit. I have been amazed at times at the different sounds and words that have manifested. The Bible never says "tongue," singular. It is always "tongues," which means there is always the chance of plurality. But I have to exercise my faith whenever I speak with tongues, because I do not know what I am going to say. I abandon myself to the Spirit of God, and let Him take it from there.

You cannot be self-conscious when you pray in the Spirit. Many people are concerned about how they will sound to other people when the thing they should be cognizant of is how they sound to their Father. He is the person they are talking to, not their wives, husbands, children, friends, or angels. The question really should be how God perceives them and receives what they are saying.

Keep praying in the spirit, and after a while, you will become accustomed to hearing yourself in your heavenly language just like you hear yourself talk in your native language. It will become exceedingly easier for you to speak with tongues, and your speaking will bless your whole life. What your spirit receives from God will help educate your soul, which contains your mind, your desires, your will, and your emotions. That in turn will help you to direct your life. I wish I had a way to convey to you the joy, assurance, faith and power I personally experience because of my praying in the Spirit — and I have no idea what I am saying when I pray.

8. *Can you be speaking with tongues, and have it turn into the gift of tongues, as referred to in 1 Corinthians 12:10?*

It is possible. There have been times when a person has been praying in the Spirit, and God will start talking to that person personally. What comes out of the person's mouth will change from speaking with tongues as the language of his or her spirit to the manifestation of the gift of divers kinds of tongues. Then the individual will interpret it out to himself or herself. That will not happen every week, every month, or every year, but it can happen nonetheless.

Understand, again, that in your private devotional time, you do not really have to know what you are saying. However, the Bible tells us in 1 Corinthians 14:13:

> **Therefore let him who speaks in a tongue pray that he may interpret.**

Paul is certainly referring there about public assembly, but what he says can also apply to private devotion. Either way, there is no one better to talk to you than yourself. Most people generally have more confidence in their own words than they do in anyone else's, because they know themselves better than they know another person. So you can pray for the interpretation in your prayer time, and the Lord may give it to you.

Where many Christians have a problem is that their word is no good and they know it. They know that when they tell someone, "I'll call you," they will not do it. They may not want to be bothered with the person anymore, but they say they will call anyway.

These Believers get into habits like that, and all those little things turn into big things over a period of time. All of it affects their spirits and souls, and after a while, they have no confidence in what they say. They may need some help in dealing with that situation, but as Jesus said in Mark 9:23, "... all things are possible to him who believes."

9. *There was one time when you and Kenneth Hagin were ministering to the people, and at one point, it sounded like you and Kenneth Hagin were speaking with tongues to one another as though you were having a conversation. What was it exactly that happened?*

The person who asked this question was pointing out something that happened when Kenneth Hagin came to Crenshaw Christian Center to hold a crusade. While he was ministering to the people, Kenneth Hagin started speaking with tongues. However, when Hagin spoke with tongues, it was not a manifestation of the gift of divers kinds of tongues. His speaking was a case of personal ministry.

When the gift of divers kinds of tongues manifests, it is usually in the context of public assembly, and it has to be interpreted so the people can know what is being said. There is also devotional tongues, when you are speaking to the Father all by yourself, building yourself up on your most holy faith. But sometimes the Lord will just do something spiritually that is a little different than what you are normally used to.

What happened at the Kenneth Hagin meeting was that Kenneth Hagin got into an area of the spirit where he could not say anything in English. He was more yielded to his spirit than he was to his mind. When you get to that point, it may appear that you do not have any control, but it is simply a case of your being more conscious of the spirit part of you than you are of the physical part of you. You become oblivious to what is happening around you physically, and everything you do is spiritually oriented.

While Kenneth Hagin was at this point in the spirit, he was ministering to a woman in a wheelchair. He spoke to me with other tongues. I spoke back to him with tongues, he spoke to me with tongues again, and I spoke back to him with tongues again. What we were actually doing was communicating in the spirit regarding that woman's condition. After Hagin and I finished speaking with tongues, I told the woman in English what Hagin had said to me in the spirit.

That was the first time anything like that had happened to me. Also, the crusade was being broadcast on a Christian television station, and many people called the station because they were shook up by what happened and could not find chapter and verse for it. But as I just said, sometimes God will do things just a little differently than usual. In John 20:30-31, we have the following recorded:

> **And truly Jesus did many other signs in the presence of His disciples, which are not written in this book;**
> **but these are written that you may believe that Jesus is the Christ, the Son of God, and that believing you may have life in His name.**

121

I want to extract a principle from these verses that will help you understand what happened at the Kenneth Hagin crusade. The principle is that when Jesus walked the earth, He had many things happen in the realm of the things of God that were simply not written down. You may ask, "How can you know when something supernatural is spiritually valid?" You can prove it very easily. All you have to do is take what is written in the Word of God and compare it to what is being manifested.

Some people will say, "We can't find any scripture in the Bible that supports what happened at that crusade." But let me respond by asking a question: Can you find a verse of scripture that says what happened at that crusade cannot happen? Two people talked to one another in the spirit, then one of the people gave the interpretation to an individual who was being ministered to. It blessed the people, it exalted the name of Jesus, and it ministered life to an individual. As long as what happened fits with the principles spelled out in the Word of God, there is nothing that says an occurrence like that cannot happen.

Let me give you an illustration to show you what I mean. On Sunday mornings, the choir ministers in song before I minister the Word of God. You can read from Matthew to Revelation and find no mention of having a choir in a local church. But there is a general principle stated in Psalm 150:6, which says, **Let everything that has breath praise the Lord.** So there is nothing wrong with having a choir minister in song in the church. There is also nothing wrong with having someone lead praise and worship. You can even have four or five people lead praise and worship, and it will not violate anything in the Word.

What I am talking about here is a matter of procedure. It is not a matter of doctrine. When it comes to espousing a particular doctrine, you have to find that specific doctrine in the Word of God. You cannot invent your own doctrine. But when it comes to procedures, there are a variety of things God leaves open for you. The Holy Spirit may lead you to do something a certain way, but the fact you never did it that way before does not make it wrong. What matters is your ability to measure it with the principles outlined in the Word. That is what is important.

10. *In Luke 10:27, just to paraphrase, it says to love the Lord with all your mind. I am just wondering, even though we know that unless we verbally speak something out, either in the spirit or in the understanding* [in our native language], *that our prayers are not answered, does anything happen to a prayer you just pray in your mind?*

First of all, I would not use the term "pray in my mind," because prayer is saying something. Jesus says in Luke 11:2, **"When you pray, say."** Jesus is our chief example of how we should pray, and every time He prayed, He said something.

I know what you mean when you say "pray in your mind," in terms of having thoughts in your mind. I can think about everything in my mind that I have already said with my mouth, but that is not praying. That is thinking, and nothing happens to it. Those thoughts stay in your mind until you verbalize them. The bottom line is going to be what you do, and prayer is not something you only think. It is something you do.

11. *On the Day of Pentecost, when the Holy Spirit was given, the Bible says there were three things that happened — (1) there was a sound as of a rushing mighty wind, (2) there were divided tongues as of fire, and (3) they spoke with other tongues. Why is it that we do not see the other two signs today with the speaking with tongues? Is it really valid to speak with tongues when you do not have the sound as of a rushing mighty wind and the cloven tongues as of fire?*

Let me deal with the divided tongues as of fire first. In Matthew 3:11, John the Baptist is speaking, and he makes this statement:

> "I indeed baptize you with water unto repentance, but He who is coming after me is mightier than I, whose sandals I am not worthy to carry. He will baptize you with the Holy Spirit and fire."

This statement is also recorded in two other Gospels. I believe it was stated by John for the benefit of the disciples who were with him, so that three and a half years later, when the Holy Spirit came and the tongues as of fire appeared, they would go back in their minds to what John had said. That way, they would recognize it was the event John was talking about — that Jesus was now the head of the Church, and had gone back to heaven to take His seat at the right hand of the Father.

It is interesting to note that after Acts 2:4, there is never anything mentioned in the Bible about fire in association with the Holy Spirit. The reason for that is that the fire was associated only with the coming of the Holy Spirit to take up His position as the power source of the Body of Christ. The Holy Spirit has been here approximately 2,000 years, so He does not need any more fire to prove His coming.

As for the sound as of a rushing mighty wind, that was just something that happened on the day the Holy Spirit came. There has been no record of that sound before or since, and the Bible does not satisfy our curiosity as to why it happened, so that sound is not something normally associated with the Holy Spirit. That sound, however, did catch the attention of the disciples, plus it was heard down the stairs going to the upper room where the disciples were located, down the street from the upper room, and throughout the neighborhood. It drew the attention of many curiosity seekers, and those curiosity seekers became Believers as a result of the Holy Spirit's manifestation.

Actually, you do not really need the fire and the sound as of a rushing mighty wind, because that was never promised to you. The Holy Spirit and the ability to speak with other tongues is what you are promised, and they are what you can receive for your spiritual edification and enrichment. The fire and the sound were a one-time transaction. You do not need them now because the Holy Spirit is already here for your benefit.

12. *Was Jesus filled with the Spirit, or was the Spirit upon Him like in the Old Testament? And if Jesus were filled with the Spirit, and He is our example, did He speak with other tongues?*

The person who asked this question also quoted Matthew 3:16, Mark 1:10, Luke 3:22, and John 1:31-32. Very briefly, those scriptures are the ones that talk about Jesus being baptized by John the Baptist in the Jordan River, and John saw the Spirit descending in a bodily shape like a dove, and descended upon Jesus.

Actually, the Holy Spirit came upon Jesus for John the Baptist's benefit. John could not see inside of Jesus to see the Holy Spirit living in Him. So when the Holy Spirit appeared at the Jordan River to anoint Jesus to stand in the office of prophet, He came down in a bodily shape and form like a dove's so that John could see what was going on. Until that happened, John did not know who the Lamb of God was.

When the Holy Spirit descended upon Jesus, He actually came inside of Him. Jesus was actually filled with the Spirit. A scripture that proves this out is John 14:8-10:

> Philip said to Him, "Lord, show us the Father, and it is sufficient for us."
>
> Jesus said to him, "Have I been with you so long, and yet you have not known Me, Philip? He who has seen Me has seen the Father; so how can you say, 'Show us the Father'?
>
> "Do you not believe that I am in the Father, and the Father in Me? The words that I speak to you I do not speak on My own authority; but the Father who dwells in Me does the works."

How did the Father do the works in and through Jesus? By the anointing and the infilling of the Holy Spirit. Therefore, this verse qualifies as a proof text for establishing the fact that Jesus was filled with the Holy Spirit.

As to the question, "Did Jesus speak with tongues?" Jesus would not have had to speak with tongues, because He was not a sinner. His communication with the Father had never been cut off like ours had been. Since Jesus already had direct communication with the Father, and had never done anything to break that communication link, He did not have to talk to the Father with other tongues out of His spirit.

13. Please explain John 20:22, when Jesus said to the disciples, "Receive the Holy Spirit." Is there any relation to this in receiving the Holy Spirit as referred to in the book of Acts?

In John 20:19-22, it says:

> **Then, the same day at evening** [this was after Jesus had been resurrected], **being the first day of the week, when the doors were shut where the disciples were assembled, for fear of the Jews, Jesus came and stood in the midst, and said to them, "Peace be with you."**
>
> **When He had said this, He showed them His hands and His side. Then the disciples were glad when they saw the Lord.**
>
> **So Jesus said to them again, "Peace to you! As the Father has sent Me, I also send you."**
>
> **And when He had said this, He breathed on them, and said to them, "Receive the Holy Spirit."**

I do not know why verse 22 is stated the way that it is, but it is obvious from the second chapter of Acts that the disciples were not filled with the Holy Spirit at that time. Number one, they did not speak with tongues. Number two, if the disciples had been filled, it would have made what happened on the day of Pentecost a farce, because the Holy Spirit would have been coming back to fill people who were already filled.

I believe that John 20:22 is referring to when the disciples were born again. It is talking about when they were saved. Forget about speaking with tongues for the moment. What is the real purpose for receiving the Holy Spirit? Supernatural power. So if Jesus said, "Receive the Holy Spirit," and they received the Holy Spirit, they would have had the power.

Keep what I just said in mind, and read John 20:26:

> And after eight days His disciples were again inside, and Thomas with them. Jesus came, the doors being shut, and stood in the midst, and said, "Peace to you!"

This was eight days after Jesus told the disciples, "Receive the Holy Spirit." Now read Acts 1:1-3:

> The former account I made, O Theophilus, of all that Jesus began both to do and teach,
> until the day in which He was taken up, after He through the Holy Spirit had given commandments to the apostles whom He had chosen,
> to whom He also presented Himself alive after His suffering by many infallible proofs, being seen by them during forty days....

Jesus was on the earth at least 40 days after He was resurrected. I am not sure whether you can add the eight days we read about in John 20:26 to the 40, or if the eight were included in the 40. Either way, it is a long time — over a month. If the disciples had truly received the Holy Spirit, they should have been filled with the Spirit all that time.

Verses three and four go on to say this:

> to whom He also presented Himself alive after His suffering by many infallible proofs, being seen by them during forty days and speaking of the things pertaining to the kingdom of God.
> And being assembled together with them, He commanded them not to depart from Jerusalem, but to wait....

You never wait for anything unless what you are waiting for has not yet come. If it has already come, there is no point in waiting. So what were the disciples supposed to wait for? According to Acts 1:4-5, they were to wait

> ... for the Promise of the Father, "which," He said, "you have heard from Me;
> "for John truly baptized with water, but you shall be baptized with the Holy Spirit not many days from now."

So there were still some more days that were going to pass before the event Jesus mentions was going to occur. Acts 1:6-8 go on to say:

> Therefore, when they had come together, they asked Him, saying, "Lord will You at this time restore the kingdom to Israel?"
> And He said to them, "It is not for you to know times or seasons which the Father has put in His own authority.
> "But you shall receive...."

Wait a minute: "You shall receive"? How could the disciples receive what they had already received? Jesus said, **"But you shall receive."** Shall is future tense. If Jesus had said, "But you have received," then the statement would be past tense, and there would be no question as to whether or not they had already received. But He did not say, "But you have received." He said, **"But you shall receive."**

> "But you shall receive power when the Holy
> Spirit has come...."

The Holy Spirit must not have already come if
Jesus says He is going to come.

> "But you shall receive power when the Holy
> Spirit has come upon you; and you shall be witnesses
> to Me in Jerusalem, and in all Judea and Samaria,
> and to the end of the earth."

The first chapter of Acts goes on to talk about
choosing someone to take Judas' place. Then we get
over to the second chapter, which begins with the
phrase, **When the Day of Pentecost had fully come.**
So the day of Pentecost had not yet come. The day of
Pentecost was 50 days after Passover.

Acts 2:1-4 tell us this:

> When the Day of Pentecost had fully come,
> they were all with one accord in one place.
> And suddenly there came a sound from
> heaven, as of a rushing mighty wind, and it filled
> the whole house where they were sitting.
> Then there appeared to them divided tongues,
> as of fire, and one sat upon each of them.
> And they were all filled with the Holy Spirit
> and began to speak with other tongues, as the
> Spirit gave them utterance.

When were the disciples filled? When the day
of Pentecost had fully come. That was more than 40
days after Jesus told them, **"Receive the Holy
Spirit."**

I believe that when Jesus told the disciples, **"Receive the Holy Spirit,"** that was actually when they became born again. You have to be a Christian in order to receive the Holy Spirit, just like you have to be a female in order to get pregnant. I do not care how many blonde, brunette or red wigs you put on, how many balloons you put inside of a bra and strap it to your chest, how many lace panties you put on, how many high-heeled shoes you wear, or how many pairs of pantyhose you put on. You cannot get pregnant unless you are a female. You may look like a woman, but you are not one unless you have the equipment with which to get pregnant.

By the same token, the disciples had to be born again before they could be eligible to be filled with the Spirit, and they could not be born again until after Jesus went to heaven and deposited His blood in the holy sanctuary there. So anytime between when Jesus came back down from placing His blood in heaven and when He ascended to heaven 40 or so days later, they could have been born again. Again, I believe they were born again when Jesus said, **"Receive the Holy Spirit."** I do not know why that terminology is used in that verse, but that is what I think happened.

14. *When or where did the other 108 disciples who were in the upper room on the Day of Pentecost receive the new birth?*

You may have read that question and thought, "What is this about, '... the other 108 disciples'?"

Usually, the first thing you think of when you hear the word *disciple* is the 12 disciples mentioned by name in the Bible. But Jesus had more than 12 disciples.

We already read John 20:19-22 earlier, but I want to point out something you may have never noticed. In verse 19, John writes:

> **Then, the same day at evening, being the first day of the week, when the doors were shut where the disciples were assembled, for fear of the Jews, Jesus came and stood in the midst, and said to them, "Peace be with you."**

Now be honest about it. All these years you may have read this verse, didn't you think of the 12 disciples we always think of, and nobody else? I know that I did before I received this question. I had never thought about the possibility of anyone else being there, but actually, all 120 of Jesus' disciples were in that room when He appeared.

John goes on to say this in verses 20 and 21:

> **When He had said this, He showed them His hands and His side. Then the disciples were glad when they saw the Lord.**
> **So Jesus said to them again, "Peace to you! As the Father has sent Me, I also send you."**

Would Jesus have been sending only 12 disciples? Probably not. The 12 disciples named in the four Gospels were only Jesus' "inner circle." We know Jesus had other disciples because on one occasion He sent 70 disciples out. Then in the upper room mentioned in Acts 2:4, there were 120 people gathered. We call them disciples, but they were students, learners, and followers.

John 20:22:

> **And when He had said this, He breathed on them, and said to them, "Receive the Holy Spirit."**

Jesus did not necessarily breathe on just the 12. He breathed on all the disciples, so they were all born again.

Right away, you might think, "They must have been in a little room. How could they have gotten 120 people in there?" In the fourth chapter of Acts, it says they were in the upper room, and that there were about 120 people, so the room must have been big enough for the 120. Also, in Luke 22:7-12, we have this statement:

> Then came the Day of Unleavened Bread, when the Passover must be killed.
> And He sent Peter and John, saying, "Go and prepare the Passover for us, that we may eat."
> So they said to Him, "Where do You want us to prepare?"
> And He said to them, "Behold, when you have entered the city, a man will meet you carrying a pitcher of water; follow him into the house which he enters.
> "Then you shall say to the master of the house, 'The Teacher says to you, "Where is the guest room where I may eat the Passover with My disciples?"'

"Then he will show you a large, furnished upper room; there make ready."

That was the room where Jesus and the disciples ate the Last Supper. When you think about all the pictures you have ever seen about the Last Supper, you usually think of nothing but a table with Jesus and the 12. You never see the rest of the disciples, but they were around.

I submit to you that this room was the same upper room the 120 were in on the Day of Pentecost. I believe that room was also the one the disciples were in when Jesus appeared to them after the resurrection, and that when Jesus breathed on the disciples and told them to "receive the Holy Ghost," that all the 120 were in there.

15. Can the Holy Spirit reveal something new to you via the gifts of the Spirit, and it not bear witness with your spirit?

Yes, absolutely. The reason what the Holy Spirit reveals may not bear witness with your spirit is that you may not be listening to Him. Many times, the Holy Spirit will say something, and we will not pay attention to what He is telling us.

A perfect example of this is when a person gets divorced after being married only a short time. The Holy Spirit told that person not to marry the person he or she married, but the individual did it anyway. Many times, the person thought, "We've already made wedding plans, and it would be an embarrassment to cancel out now," or "We knew it, but we'd already spent all of this money on the wedding."

I told my daughters when they were planning their weddings not to worry about the money, that right up to the time I said, "Do you take this man," they could say, "No, daddy, I think I've changed my mind," and it would be fine with me. I wanted their happiness more than I wanted the money. After all, God supplies all my needs, so I can be blessed with more money.

What is worse or more embarrassing — not going through with the wedding, or a divorce or annulment? Or to be saddled with three kids and no father? That is why the Holy Spirit tries to warn us — not to keep us from doing something, but to tell us that what we want to do may be a big mistake.

8

How You Can Be Filled
With the Holy Spirit

You may have read this book on the Holy Spirit, and even thought before now that you were filled with the Spirit. But since reading this book, you may have come to the realization that you were never really filled with the Spirit after all. If that is the case, and you want to receive the gift of the Holy Spirit, here are some steps you will want to follow.

POINT ONE: The first thing you must make sure of — and it is essential if you want to be filled with the Spirit — is that you have to have accepted Jesus Christ as your personal Savior and Lord. The Bible tells us in John 7:38-39 that the promise of the Holy Spirit is made only to Believers. By no means should anyone who is not a Believer pray for the gift of the Holy Spirit. Here are some Scriptures you can check to be sure of your salvation:

John 1:12	John 5:24	Ephesians 2:8-9
John 3:3, 5	John 6:47	Acts 16:31
John 3:16, 18, 36	John 20:31	

If you read these scriptures and say to yourself, "I do not know if that is me or not," or "No, I know that is not me. I have never received Jesus," here is how simple it is to be saved. Paul tells us in Romans 10:9-10:

> that if you confess with your mouth the Lord Jesus and believe in your heart that God has raised Him from the dead, you will be saved.
> For with the heart one believes unto righteousness, and with the mouth confession is made unto salvation.

Do you believe that God raised Jesus Christ from the dead? Have you confessed Jesus as the Lord of your life? If you have not confessed Him, and would like to, pray the following prayer aloud:

> "Dear God, You said in Romans 10:9-10 that if I confess with my mouth the Lord Jesus and believe in my heart that God raised Him from the dead, I will be saved.
> "I believe that Jesus Christ is your Son, and that He was sent into the world to redeem my life. I believe that He died for me, and that He was raised from the dead for my justification. Jesus, be the Lord over my life. I confess You now as my Savior and Lord, and I do believe it with my heart. According to Your Word, I have now become the righteousness of God in Christ, and I am now saved. Thank You, Jesus. Amen."

In Romans 10:13, Paul says, **For "whoever calls on the name of the Lord shall be saved."** You have called on the name of the Lord, so salvation is yours now, and the scriptures listed under POINT ONE now apply to you. Confess them as yours, believe and receive.

POINT TWO: Read the Book of Acts and 1 Corinthians, chapters 12-14, and let the Word show you that the Holy Spirit is meant for every Believer today. Then read the following passages of Scripture carefully:

Joel 2:28-29	Mark 1:8	Luke 11:9-13
Matthew 3:11	John 1:33	Luke 24:49
Luke 3:16	Mark 16:17	

God says that in the last days He will pour out His Spirit upon all flesh. There is no expiration date or statute of limitation. All who seek the Holy Spirit may find Him.

POINT THREE: Remember that the gift of the Holy Spirit is not given as an attainment or reward, based on some supposed degree of holiness. It is based solely on the fact that Jesus promised to give Him to every Believer, freely and by grace. Below are some scriptures you may want to check:

John 7:38-39	John 14:25-26	John 16:12-14
John 14:16-17	John 15:16	John 16:7

POINT FOUR: When you receive the gift of the Holy Spirit, it helps to be with a group of Spirit-filled Christians who can instruct, encourage and pray with you. Although it is not essential, I personally find it to be a great help for two specific reasons. First, it is scriptural. Acts 8:17, 9:17, and 19:6 show us how others can help us by the laying on of hands as a point of faith release. Second, Satan will immediately challenge you as to the authenticity of your experience, so it is good to have the witness of Christians who can affirm what has happened to you.

POINT FIVE: Now that you are ready to receive, simply pray this prayer of invitation:

> **"Father, I believe with all my heart, based on the Scriptures, that the gift of the Holy Spirit is meant for me. Just as I have trusted You for my eternal salvation by faith, so now do I trust You, by faith, to give me the fullness of the Holy Spirit with the evidence of speaking with other tongues. I now receive, by faith, the gift of the Holy Spirit. Thank You in Jesus' Name, Amen."**

POINT SIX: By faith, open your mouth and yield your tongue to the Holy Spirit. Praise the Lord in tongues as the Spirit gives you the utterance. Remember, the Holy Spirit does not do the speaking — you do. Initiate syllables with your tongue and lips. Often unfamiliar words will flash into your mind. Speak them out in praise to the Lord. The more yielded and believing you become, the more fluent and free your language will become.

If at first your language does not "flow," do not become discouraged or doubt that you received the gift of the Holy Spirit. The devil may suggest to you that you are making it all up, but do not listen to him.

Remember, the devil is a liar and the father of lies. Continue stepping out in faith by yielding your voice to the Lord.

POINT SEVEN: Continue to exercise your gift daily. Like an athlete preparing for competition, you must "stay in shape" by giving your new experience a daily workout. Keep praying and singing in the spirit. If at all possible, seek other Spirit-filled Christians to associate with. And above all, find yourself a Spirit-filled church that is teaching the uncompromising, full-counsel of God. That is the way to grow and stay ahead of the devil.

It is also important for you to study the Bible daily on your own. That way, the Spirit of God can educate you through the Word on the will of God and the various aspects of victorious living. I cannot emphasize the following point strongly enough: YOU NEED THE WORD *AND* THE HOLY SPIRIT to succeed in fighting "the good fight of faith" (1 Tim. 6:12). Being filled with the Spirit is not the end of all spiritual revelation. It is only the beginning.

Epilogue

When you allow the Holy Spirit to lead and teach you, you will not only gain revelation knowledge, but you will have the potential of becoming a powerful and effective witness for Jesus Christ. For this reason, plus all the others I have mentioned in this book, the devil will try to intimidate you, and try to rob you of God's best. Do not let him do that!

The Holy Spirit is here solely for our benefit. We need His power, wisdom and guidance so we can overcome what the enemy throws at us at every turn. That was why Jesus told His disciples in Acts 1:4-5 to **wait for the Promise of the Father, "which," He said, "you have heard from Me; for John truly baptized with water, but you shall be baptized with the Holy Spirit not many days from now."** Jesus knew His disciples would need the Holy Spirit for them to succeed in their lives and ministries — and that need has not changed from that time to the present.

God has not put anything superfluous into the Body of Christ. Therefore, if He gave us the Holy Spirit, He did so for a reason. We need to exercise wisdom to find out why God gave Him to us, and we should have enough common sense, spiritually speaking, to take advantage of the situation. The Holy Spirit is here to teach us, guide us, assist us. He is the Helper every Believer needs.

About the Author

Dr. Frederick K.C. Price is the founder and pastor of Crenshaw Christian Center in Los Angeles, California and Crenshaw Christian Center East in Manhattan, New York. He is known worldwide as a teacher of the biblical principles of faith, healing, prosperity and the Holy Spirit. During his more than 50 years in ministry, countless lives have been changed by his dynamic and insightful teachings that truly "tell it like it is."

His television program, *Ever Increasing Faith (EIF)*, has been broadcast throughout the world for more than 25 years and currently airs in 15 of the 20 largest markets in America, reaching an audience of more than 15 million households each week. *EIF* is also, webcast on the Internet via www.faithdome.org. The *EIF* radio program is heard on stations across the world, including the continent of Europe via short-wave radio.

Author of more than 50 popular books teaching practical application of biblical principles, Dr. Price pastors one of America's largest church congregations, with a membership of approximately 22,000. The Los Angeles church sanctuary, the FaithDome, is among the most notable and largest in the nation, with seating capacity of more than 10,000.

In 1990, Dr. Price founded the Fellowship of Inner-City Word of Faith Ministries (FICWFM). Members of FICWFM include more than 300 churches from all over the United States and various countries. The Fellowship, which meets regionally throughout the year and hosts an annual convention, is not a denomination. Its mission is to provide fellowship, leadership, guidance and a spiritual covering for those desiring a standard of excellence in ministry. Members share methods and experiences commonly faced by ministries in the inner cities. Their focus is how to apply the Word of Faith to solve their challenges.

Dr. Price holds an honorary Doctorate of Divinity degree from Oral Roberts University and an honorary diploma from Rhema Bible Training Center.

On September 6, 2000, Dr. Price was the first black pastor to speak at Town Hall Los Angeles. He is the recipient of two prestigious awards. He is a 1998 recipient of the Horatio Alger Award. Each year, this prestigious honor is bestowed upon ten "outstanding Americans who exemplify inspirational success, triumph over adversity, and an uncommon commitment to helping others ...." He also received the 1998 Southern Christian Leadership Conference's Kelly Miller Smith Interfaith Award. This award is given to clergy who have made the most significant contribution through religious expression affecting the nation and the world.

Books by
Frederick K.C. Price, D.D.

WHY SHOULD CHRISTIANS SUFFER?

FAITH WORDS THAT WOW!

EVER INCREASING FAITH STUDY JOURNAL
A Recorded Treasury of Personal Study Notes

GROWING IN GOD'S WORD:
Devotional & Prayer Journal

THE PURPOSE OF PROSPERITY

INTEGRITY
The Guarantee for Success

HIGHER FINANCE
How to Live Debt-Free

RACE, RELIGION & RACISM, VOLUME 1
A Bold Encounter With Division in the Church

RACE, RELIGION & RACISM, VOLUME 2
Perverting the Gospel to Subjugate a People

RACE, RELIGION & RACISM, VOLUME 3
Jesus, Christianity and Islam

THE TRUTH ABOUT ... THE BIBLE

THE TRUTH ABOUT ... DEATH

THE TRUTH ABOUT ... DISASTERS

THE TRUTH ABOUT ... FATE

THE TRUTH ABOUT ... FEAR

THE TRUTH ABOUT ... HOMOSEXUALITY

THE TRUTH ABOUT ... RACE

THE TRUTH ABOUT ... WORRY

THE TRUTH ABOUT ... GIVING

LIVING IN HOSTILE TERRITORY
A Survival Guide for the Overcoming Christian

DR. PRICE'S GOLDEN NUGGETS
A Treasury of Wisdom for Both Ministers and Laypeople

BUILDING ON A FIRM FOUNDATION

FIVE LITTLE FOXES OF FAITH

THE CHRISTIAN FAMILY:
Practical Insight for Family Living

IDENTIFIED WITH CHRIST:
A Complete Cycle From Defeat to Victory

THE CHASTENING OF THE LORD

TESTING THE SPIRITS

BEWARE! THE LIES OF SATAN

THE WAY, THE WALK,
AND THE WARFARE OF THE BELIEVER
(A Verse-by-Verse Study on the Book of Ephesians)

THREE KEYS TO POSITIVE CONFESSION

THE PROMISED LAND
(A New Era for the Body of Christ)

A NEW LAW FOR A NEW PEOPLE

THE VICTORIOUS, OVERCOMING LIFE
(A Verse-by-Verse Study on the Book of Colossians)

149

To receive Dr. Price's book and tape catalog
or be placed on the EIF mailing list,
please call:

(800) 927-3436

*Books are also available
at local bookstores everywhere.*

For more information, please write:

**Crenshaw Christian Center
P.O. Box 90000
Los Angeles, CA 90009**

or check your local TV or Webcast listing:

Ever Increasing Faith Ministries

or visit our Website:

<u>www.faithdome.org</u>